Taste *of* Home

SOUPS

TASTE OF HOME BOOKS • RDA ENTHUSIAST BRANDS, LLC • MILWAUKEE, WI

Taste of Home

EDITORIAL

Editor-in-Chief: Catherine Cassidy

Vice President, Content Operations: Kerri Balliet
Creative Director: Howard Greenberg

Managing Editor, Print & Digital Books: Mark Hagen
Associate Creative Director: Edwin Robles Jr.

Editors: Hazel Wheaton, Christine Rukavena
Art Directors: Maggie Conners, Raeann Thompson
Layout Designer: Catherine Fletcher
Editorial Production Manager: Dena Ahlers
Editorial Production Coordinator: Jill Banks
Copy Chief: Deb Warlaumont Mulvey
Copy Editor: Ellie Piper
Contributing Copy Editor: Kristin Sutter
Editorial Intern: Maddie Rashid
Editorial Services Administrator: Marie Brannon

Content Director: Julie Blume Benedict
Senior Digital Editor: Kelsey Mueller
Food Editors: Gina Nistico; James Schend;
Peggy Woodward, RDN
Recipe Editors: Sue Ryon (lead), Irene Yeh

Test Kitchen & Food Styling Manager:
Sarah Thompson
Test Cooks: Nicholas Iverson (lead), Matthew Hass
Food Stylists: Kathryn Conrad (lead),
Lauren Knoelke, Shannon Roum
Prep Cooks: Bethany Van Jacobson (lead),
Melissa Hansen, Aria C. Thornton
Culinary Team Assistant: Maria Petrella

Photography Director: Stephanie Marchese
Photographers: Dan Roberts, Jim Wieland
Photographer/Set Stylist: Grace Natoli Sheldon
Set Stylists: Melissa Franco (lead), Stacey Genaw,
Dee Dee Jacq
Set Stylist Assistant: Stephanie Chojnacki

Business Architect, Publishing Technologies:
Amanda Harmatys
Solutions Architect, Publishing Technologies:
John Mosey
Business Analyst, Publishing Technologies:
Kate Unger
Junior Business Analyst, Publishing Technologies:
Shannon Stroud

Editorial Business Manager: Kristy Martin
Rights & Permissions Associate:
Samantha Lea Stoeger
Editorial Business Associate: Andrea Meiers

BUSINESS

Vice President, Group Publisher: Kirsten Marchioli
Publisher: Donna Lindskog
**Business Development Director, Taste of Home
Live:** Laurel Osman
**Promotional Partnerships Manager, Taste of Home
Live:** Jamie Piette Andrzejewski

TRUSTED MEDIA BRANDS, INC.

President & Chief Executive Officer:
Bonnie Kintzer

Chief Financial Officer: Dean Durbin
Chief Marketing Officer: C. Alec Casey
Chief Revenue Officer: Richard Sutton
Chief Digital Officer: Vince Errico
**Senior Vice President, Global HR &
Communications:**
Phyllis E. Gebhardt, SPHR; SHRM-SCP
General Counsel: Mark Sirota
Vice President, Magazine Marketing:
Christopher Gaydos
Vice President, Operations: Michael Garzone
Vice President, Consumer Marketing Planning:
Jim Woods
Vice President, Digital Product & Technology:
Nick Contardo
Vice President, Financial Planning & Analysis:
William Houston
Publishing Director, Books: Debra Polansky

For other *Taste of Home* books and products,
visit us at **tasteofhome.com.**

International Standard Book Number:
978-1-61765-613-2
Library of Congress Control Number: 2016952314

Cover Photographer: Jim Wieland
Set Stylist: Stacey Genaw
Food Stylist: Kathryn Conrad

Pictured on title page: Cream of Cauliflower Soup,
page 95

Pictured on front cover: Slow Cooker Turkey Chili,
page 141

Pictured on spine: Loaded Potato Soup, page 16

Pictured on back cover (left to right): So Easy Gazpacho,
page 187; The Best Chicken & Dumplings, page 36

Printed in China.
1 3 5 7 9 10 8 6 4 2

GET SOCIAL WITH US

To find a recipe tasteofhome.com
To submit a recipe tasteofhome.com/submit
To find out about other *Taste of Home* products shoptasteofhome.

 **LIKE US**
facebook.com/tasteofhome

 **PIN US**
pinterest.com/taste_of_home

 FOLLOW US
@tasteofhome

 TWEET US
twitter.com/tasteofhor

Roasted Tomato Bisque, page 107
Quinoa Turkey Chili, page 150

The Ultimate
Comfort Food

Soup is a magic food. It has become a symbol of healing for both the body and the soul. The original melting pot, soup is a dish that brings friends and families together. In every culture around the world, there has been a richly flavored pot simmering above a fire.

For the home cook, the beauty of soup is its versatility. A soup is a great way to feed a large family or a party of two. Make a big pot of soup on Sunday night, and you'll feast on the leftovers for the rest of the week—especially since soups are often even better on the second day. Soup can lead off the meal as an appetizer, be a main course when served with a salad or a big hunk of crusty bread or even make a surprising appearance as a cool, sweet dessert.

Now *Taste of Home Soups* brings you 100 recipes that let you explore a wide range of options, from elegant bisques to hearty stews to refreshing chilled delights. Get ready to dive in, try new recipes and fill your bowl!

Try this
**Bean &
Butternut
Soup,**
page 56.

Navy
Bean Soup,
page 19

Fresh Corn &
Potato Chowder,
page 116

STOCK YOUR PANTRY!

When it comes to pulling together a fantastic soup, having core ingredients on hand is essential. With these staples in the pantry, you can create your own masterpiece on short notice.

BROTHS/STOCKS:
Chicken, beef and/or vegetable

HERBS/SPICES/SEASONINGS:
Spices/Seasonings: Peppercorns, bay leaf, kosher salt, Worcestershire sauce
Dried herbs: Basil, coriander, cumin, oregano, rosemary, sage, tarragon, thyme

FRESH VEGETABLES:
Carrots, celery, garlic, onions, potatoes

OILS:
Olive oil, canola oil

CANNED GOODS:
Tomatoes: Crushed or diced, sauce, paste
Beans: Kidney beans, black beans, white beans (great northern, cannellini, navy)

NONPERISHABLES:
Dried lentils, dried beans, pasta, noodles, rice (long grain white and/or brown)

A BIT OF HEAT:
Hot pepper sauce, chili powder, cayenne pepper, red pepper flakes

5 TIPS FOR GREAT SOUP

1. The flavors in many soups—meat (especially meat on the bone), garlic, onion and bay leaves—benefit from long cooking times. Give your soup plenty of time to simmer.

2. Some ingredients lose their flavor with extended heating. Add any ingredients with dynamic flavors, such as fresh herbs, later in the cooking process.

3. Salt teases out the ingredients' flavors, so add a small amount early in the cooking process. But cooking concentrates salt's flavor, so be sparing to start, and salt to taste just before serving.

4. Dress up your soup with a garnish, such as chopped nuts or fresh herbs, slivered fresh vegetables, sliced green onions, croutons, shredded cheese or crumbled bacon. A drizzle of flavored oil makes a simple and elegant finish.

5. Most savory soups are even better the next day. If time permits, make your soup the day before serving.

ALL-TIME
CLASSICS

CORN CHOWDER

I've had this chowder recipe for more than 30 years, and the whole family really enjoys its cheesy corn taste. It makes a big pot— definitely enough for seconds.

—LOLA COMER MARYSVILLE, WA

PREP: 30 MIN. • **COOK:** 30 MIN.
MAKES: 15 SERVINGS (3¾ QUARTS)

- 6 **bacon strips, chopped**
- ¾ **cup chopped sweet onion**
- 2½ **cups water**
- 2½ **cups cubed peeled potatoes**
- 2 **cups sliced fresh carrots**
- 2 **teaspoons chicken bouillon granules**
- 3 **cans (11 ounces each) gold and white corn, drained**
- ½ **teaspoon pepper**
- 7 **tablespoons all-purpose flour**
- 5 **cups 2% milk**
- 3 **cups shredded cheddar cheese**
- 1 **cup cubed process cheese (Velveeta)**

1. In a Dutch oven, cook bacon and onion over medium heat until the onion is tender. Add the water, potatoes, carrots and bouillon; bring to a boil. Reduce heat; cover and simmer for 15-20 minutes or until the potatoes are tender.

2. Stir in corn and pepper. In a large bowl, whisk flour and milk until smooth; add to the soup. Bring to a boil; cook and stir for 2 minutes or until thickened. Reduce heat. Add the cheeses; cook and stir until melted.

OH-SO-GOOD CHICKEN SOUP

I came up with this soup one weekend when my wife and I were hungry for something better than the standard. The first attempt turned out fantastic, and now I've got the recipe down to 20 minutes.
—**CHRIS DALTON** MUNDELEIN, IL

START TO FINISH: 30 MIN. • **MAKES:** 6 SERVINGS

- **4** cans (14½ ounces each) reduced-sodium chicken broth
- **2** cups uncooked bow tie pasta
- **1** tablespoon olive oil
- **1** pound boneless skinless chicken breasts, cut into ½-inch strips
- **4** green onions, chopped
- **1** pound fresh asparagus, cut into 1-inch pieces
- **1½** cups sliced fresh shiitake mushrooms
- **1** garlic clove, minced
- **⅛** teaspoon pepper
- **6** tablespoons shredded Parmesan cheese

1. In a large saucepan, bring broth to a boil. Stir in pasta; return to a boil. Reduce heat; simmer, covered, 8-10 minutes or until pasta is tender, stirring occasionally.

2. Meanwhile, in a large skillet, heat oil over medium-high heat. Add chicken and green onions; cook and stir 5 minutes. Add asparagus, mushrooms and garlic; cook and stir for 2-3 minutes or until chicken is no longer pink and asparagus is crisp-tender. Sprinkle with pepper.

3. Add chicken mixture to pasta mixture; heat through. Sprinkle with cheese.

FREEZE OPTION *Before adding cheese, cool the soup. Freeze soup and cheese separately in freezer containers. To use, partially thaw soup in refrigerator overnight. Heat through in a saucepan, stirring occasionally and adding a little broth if necessary. Sprinkle with cheese.*

PASTA E FAGIOLI

This soup can serve as a whole meal just on its own. It's delicious, hearty and healthy. I receive many compliments whenever I make it for guests.

—PENNY L. NOVY BUFFALO GROVE, IL

PREP: 30 MIN. • **COOK:** 7½ HOURS
MAKES: 8 SERVINGS (2½ QUARTS)

- 1 **pound ground beef**
- 1 **medium onion, chopped**
- 1 **carton (32 ounces) chicken broth**
- 2 **cans (14½ ounces each) diced tomatoes, undrained**
- 1 **can (15 ounces) white kidney or cannellini beans, rinsed and drained**
- 2 **medium carrots, chopped**
- 1½ **cups finely chopped cabbage**
- 1 **celery rib, chopped**
- 2 **tablespoons minced fresh basil or 2 teaspoons dried basil**
- 2 **garlic cloves, minced**
- ½ **teaspoon salt**
- ½ **teaspoon pepper**
- 1 **cup ditalini or other small pasta**
  Grated Parmesan cheese, optional

1. In a large skillet, cook beef and onion over medium heat until beef is no longer pink and onion is tender; drain.

2. Transfer to a 4- or 5-qt. slow cooker. Stir in the broth, tomatoes, beans, carrots, cabbage, celery, basil, garlic, salt and pepper. Cover and cook on low for 7-8 hours or until vegetables are tender.

3. Stir in pasta. Cover and cook on high 30 minutes longer or until pasta is tender. Sprinkle with cheese if desired.

CHUNKY BEEF & VEGETABLE SOUP

Nothing cures the winter gloom like soup, including this beefy one I first cooked up on a snowy day. Serve with crusty bread or rolls.
—**BILLY HENSLEY** MOUNT CARMEL, TN

PREP: 25 MIN. • **COOK:** 2¾ HOURS
MAKES: 8 SERVINGS (3 QUARTS)

- 1½ **pounds beef stew meat, cut into ½-inch pieces**
- 1 **teaspoon salt, divided**
- 1 **teaspoon salt-free seasoning blend, divided**
- ¾ **teaspoon pepper, divided**
- 2 **tablespoons olive oil, divided**
- 4 **large carrots, sliced**
- 1 **large onion, chopped**
- 1 **medium sweet red pepper, chopped**
- 1 **medium green pepper, chopped**
- 2 **garlic cloves, minced**
- 1 **cup Burgundy wine or additional reduced-sodium beef broth**
- 4 **cups reduced-sodium beef broth**
- 1 **can (14½ ounces) diced tomatoes, undrained**
- 2 **tablespoons tomato paste**
- 2 **tablespoons Worcestershire sauce**
- 1 **bay leaf**
- 4 **medium potatoes (about 2 pounds), cut into ½-inch cubes**

1. Sprinkle beef with ½ teaspoon each salt, seasoning blend and pepper. In a Dutch oven, heat 1 tablespoon oil over medium heat. Brown beef in batches. Remove from pot.

2. In same Dutch oven, heat remaining oil over medium heat. Add carrots, onion and peppers; cook and stir until carrots are crisp-tender. Add garlic; cook 1 minute longer.

3. Add wine, stirring to loosen browned bits from the pot. Stir in broth, tomatoes, tomato paste, Worcestershire sauce, bay leaf and remaining seasonings. Return beef to pot; bring to a boil. Reduce heat; simmer, covered, 2 hours.

4. Add potatoes; cook 30-40 minutes longer or until beef and potatoes are tender. Skim fat and discard bay leaf.

SPLIT PEA SOUP WITH HAM

PREP: 15 MIN. • **COOK:** 8 HOURS
MAKES: 7 SERVINGS (ABOUT 2 QUARTS)

- **1 can (49½ ounces) chicken broth**
- **1½ pounds smoked ham hocks**
- **2 cups each chopped onions, celery and carrots**
- **1 package (16 ounces) dried green split peas**
- **2 bay leaves**
- **Salad croutons, optional**

1. In a 4- or 5-qt. slow cooker, combine the broth, ham hocks, vegetables, split peas and bay leaves. Cover and cook on low for 8-10 hours or until ham hocks and peas are tender.

2. Discard the bay leaves. Remove meat from bones when cool enough to handle; cut ham into small pieces and set aside. Cool soup slightly.

3. In a blender, cover and process soup in batches until smooth. Return soup to slow cooker; stir in reserved ham. Heat through. Garnish with croutons if desired.

> Just let this soup simmer while you are out for the day and a delicious dinner will be ready by the time you get home. The ham hocks lend a smoky flavor.
>
> —*TASTE OF HOME* TEST KITCHEN

LOADED POTATO SOUP

I like to put a twist on my grandmother's recipes, as I did with this one. I look forward to passing my own delicious comfort food recipes down to my kids.

—**JAMIE CHASE** RISING SUN, IN

PREP: 30 MIN. • **COOK:** 8¼ HOURS
MAKES: 12 SERVINGS (4 QUARTS)

- 5 **pounds potatoes, peeled and cubed (about 10 cups)**
- 1 **medium onion, finely chopped**
- 5 **cans (14½ ounces each) chicken broth**
- 1 **garlic clove, minced**
- 1½ **teaspoons salt**
- ¼ **teaspoon pepper**
- 2 **packages (8 ounces each) cream cheese, softened and cubed**
- 1 **cup half-and-half cream**
- ¼ **cup butter, cubed**

TOPPINGS

- 1 **pound bacon strips, cooked and crumbled**
- ¾ **cup shredded sharp cheddar cheese**
- ¼ **cup minced chives**

1. Place potatoes and onion in a 6-qt. slow cooker; add broth, garlic, salt and pepper. Cook, covered, on low for 8-10 hours or until the potatoes are tender.

2. Mash potatoes to desired consistency. Stir in cream cheese, cream and butter. Cook, covered, 15 minutes longer or until heated through.

3. Just before serving, whisk soup to combine. Top each serving with bacon, cheese and chives.

NAVY BEAN SOUP

I use thrifty dried beans and a ham hock to create this comfort-food classic. Bean soup is a family favorite that I make often.
—**MILDRED LEWIS** TEMPLE, TX

PREP: 30 MIN. + SOAKING • **COOK:** 1¾ HOURS
MAKES: 10 SERVINGS (2½ QUARTS)

- 3 **cups (1½ pounds) dried navy beans**
- 1 **can (14½ ounces) diced tomatoes, undrained**
- 1 **large onion, chopped**
- 1 **meaty ham hock or 1 cup diced cooked ham**
- 2 **cups chicken broth**
- 2½ **cups water**
  Salt and pepper to taste
  Minced fresh parsley

1. Rinse and sort beans; soak according to package directions.

2. Drain and rinse beans, discarding the liquid. Place in a Dutch oven. Add the tomatoes with juice, onion, ham hock, broth, water, salt and pepper. Bring to a boil. Reduce heat; cover and simmer until beans are tender, about 1½ hours.

3. Add more water if necessary. Remove ham hock and let it stand until cool enough to handle. Remove meat from bone; discard bone. Cut meat into bite-size pieces; set aside. (For a thicker soup, let it cool slightly, puree some of the beans in a food processor or blender and return to the pot.) Return ham to soup and heat through. Garnish with parsley.

NOTES

SEAFOOD BISQUE

START TO FINISH: 30 MIN. • **MAKES:** 10 SERVINGS (2½ QUARTS)

- 2 cans (10¾ ounces each) condensed cream of mushroom soup, undiluted
- 1 can (10¾ ounces) condensed cream of celery soup, undiluted
- 2⅔ cups 2% milk
- 4 green onions, chopped
- ½ cup finely chopped celery
- 1 garlic clove, minced
- 1 teaspoon Worcestershire sauce
- ¼ teaspoon hot pepper sauce
- 1½ pounds uncooked medium shrimp, peeled and deveined
- 1 can (6 ounces) crabmeat, drained, flaked and cartilage removed
- 1 jar (4½ ounces) whole mushrooms, drained
- 3 tablespoons Madeira wine or chicken broth
- ½ teaspoon salt
- ½ teaspoon pepper
  Thinly sliced green onions, optional

In a Dutch oven, combine the first eight ingredients. Bring to a boil. Reduce heat; add the shrimp, crab and mushrooms. Simmer, uncovered, for 10 minutes. Stir in the wine, salt and pepper; cook 2-3 minutes longer. Top with onions if desired.

We live on the Gulf Coast where fresh seafood is plentiful. I adapted several recipes to create this bisque. It can be made with shrimp, crab or both.

—**PAT EDWARDS** DAUPHIN ISLAND, AL

HELPFUL HINT

Barley absorbs a lot of soup broth. If the leftovers are too thick, add extra chicken, beef or vegetable broth while reheating to achieve the desired consistency.

BEEF AND BARLEY SOUP

I came across this recipe years ago in a recipe exchange through a church group. The contributor didn't sign her name, so I don't know who to thank. But my husband and son thank me for preparing it by helping themselves to seconds and thirds!
—ELLEN MCCLEARY SCOTLAND, ON

PREP: 10 MIN. • **COOK:** 1 HOUR
MAKES: 12 SERVINGS (3 QUARTS)

- 1½ **pounds ground beef**
- 3 **celery ribs, sliced**
- 1 **medium onion, chopped**
- 3 **cans (10½ ounces each) condensed beef consomme, undiluted**
- 1 **can (28 ounces) diced tomatoes, undrained**
- 4 **medium carrots, sliced**
- 2 **cups water**
- 1 **can (10¾ ounces) condensed tomato soup, undiluted**
- ½ **cup medium pearl barley**
- 1 **bay leaf**

In a Dutch oven, cook the beef, celery and onion over medium heat until the meat is no longer pink; drain. Add the remaining ingredients; bring to a boil. Reduce heat; simmer, uncovered, for 45-50 minutes or until the barley is tender. Discard the bay leaf.

ITALIAN WEDDING SOUP

START TO FINISH: 30 MIN.
MAKES: 6 SERVINGS

- 1 package (19½ ounces) Italian turkey sausage links, casings removed
- 2 shallots, finely chopped
- 3 garlic cloves, minced
- 1 carton (32 ounces) reduced-sodium chicken broth
- ¾ cup uncooked whole wheat orzo pasta
- ¼ teaspoon pepper
- 10 cups coarsely chopped escarole or spinach
- ½ cup coarsely chopped fresh Italian parsley

1. In a 6-qt. stockpot, cook sausage, shallots and garlic over medium heat or 6-8 minutes or until sausage is no longer pink, breaking up sausage into crumbles. Drain.

2. Add broth to sausage mixture; bring to a boil. Stir in orzo, pepper and escarole; return to a boil. Reduce heat; simmer, uncovered, 10-12 minutes or until orzo is tender. Stir in parsley before serving.

My husband and I had an amazing soup with orzo in an Italian restaurant. I tweaked it to make it healthier but kept the warm, comforting flavor.

—**BARBARA SPITZER** LODI, CA

CHEDDAR CHEESE & BEER SOUP

The taste of the beer is subtle, but it's just enough to complement the cheese in this rich and creamy soup. For a slightly sweeter version, use apple juice instead of beer.
—**HOLLY LEWIS** SWINK, CO

PREP: 15 MIN. • **COOK:** 25 MIN. • **MAKES:** 6 SERVINGS

- ¼ **cup butter, cubed**
- ¾ **pound potatoes, peeled and chopped (about 2 cups)**
- 4 **celery ribs, chopped (about 2 cups)**
- 2 **medium onions, chopped (about 1½ cups)**
- 2 **medium carrots, sliced (about 1 cup)**
- ½ **cup all-purpose flour**
- 1½ **teaspoons salt**
- 1 **teaspoon ground mustard**
- ⅛ **teaspoon cayenne pepper**
- 3 **cups chicken stock**
- 3 **cups shredded sharp cheddar cheese**
- 2 **cups 2% milk**
- ½ **cup beer or apple juice**

1. In a 6-qt. stockpot, heat butter over medium-high heat. Add potatoes, celery, onions and carrots; cook and stir for 5-7 minutes or until onions are tender.
2. Stir in flour, salt, mustard and cayenne until blended; gradually stir in stock. Bring to a boil, stirring occasionally. Reduce heat; simmer, uncovered, for 10-12 minutes or until potatoes are tender. Add remaining ingredients; cook and stir until cheese is melted.

ALPHABET SOUP

Bite-size meatballs made from ground turkey perk up this fun alphabet soup. A variety of vegetables mix in a rich tomato broth seasoned with herbs.

—*TASTE OF HOME* TEST KITCHEN

PREP: 20 MIN. • **COOK:** 35 MIN. • **MAKES:** 9 SERVINGS

- 1 large egg, lightly beaten
- 2 tablespoons quick-cooking oats
- 2 tablespoons grated Parmesan cheese
- ¼ teaspoon garlic powder
- ¼ teaspoon Italian seasoning
- ½ pound lean ground turkey
- 1 cup chopped onion
- 1 cup chopped celery
- 1 cup chopped carrots
- 1 cup diced peeled potatoes
- 1 tablespoon olive oil
- 2 garlic cloves, minced
- 4 cans (14½ ounces each) reduced-sodium chicken broth
- 1 can (28 ounces) diced tomatoes, undrained
- 1 can (6 ounces) tomato paste
- ¼ cup minced fresh parsley
- 1 teaspoon dried basil
- 1 teaspoon dried thyme
- ¾ cup uncooked alphabet pasta

1. In a bowl, combine the first five ingredients. Crumble ground turkey over the mixture and mix well. Shape into ½-in. balls. In a nonstick skillet, brown meatballs in small batches over medium heat until no longer pink. Remove from the heat; set aside.

2. In a large saucepan or Dutch oven, saute the onion, celery, carrots and potatoes in oil for 5 minutes or until crisp-tender. Add garlic; saute for 1 minute longer. Add broth, tomatoes, tomato paste, parsley, basil and thyme; bring to a boil. Add pasta; cook for 5-6 minutes. Reduce heat; add meatballs. Simmer, uncovered, for 15-20 minutes or until the vegetables are tender.

CHICKEN TORTILLA SOUP

Anaheim peppers, jalapenos and cayenne add spice in this full-flavored tortilla soup.

—JOHNNA JOHNSON
SCOTTSDALE, AZ

PREP: 30 MIN. + STANDING
COOK: 45 MIN.
MAKES: 10 SERVINGS (2¾ QUARTS)

- **6 Anaheim peppers**
- **3 tablespoons canola oil, divided**
- **8 corn tortillas (6 inches), cut into ½-inch strips**
- **2 medium onions, chopped**
- **8 garlic cloves, peeled**
- **7 cups chicken broth**
- **1 can (29 ounces) tomato puree**
- **2 tablespoons minced fresh cilantro**
- **1 tablespoon ground cumin**
- **1 teaspoon ground coriander**
- **1 bay leaf**
- **2 jalapeno peppers, seeded and finely chopped, optional**
- **1 pound boneless skinless chicken breasts, cut into ½-inch cubes**
- **2 tablespoons lemon juice**
- **½ teaspoon salt**
- **¼ teaspoon pepper**
  Dash cayenne pepper
- **1½ cups shredded cheddar cheese**
- **1 medium ripe avocado, peeled and chopped**

1. Place the Anaheim peppers on a foil-lined baking sheet. Broil peppers 4 in. from heat until the skins blister, about 5 minutes. With tongs, rotate peppers a quarter turn. Broil and rotate until all sides are blistered and blackened. Immediately place peppers in a large bowl; let stand, covered, 20 minutes.

2. Peel off and discard the charred skin. Remove stems and seeds. Coarsely chop peppers; set aside.

3. Heat 2 tablespoons oil in a large skillet. Fry tortilla strips in batches until crisp and browned. Remove with a slotted spoon; drain on paper towels.

4. In a Dutch oven, heat 2 teaspoons oil over medium-high heat. Add onions; cook and stir until tender. Add garlic; cook and stir 1 minute longer. Add broth, tomato puree, cilantro, cumin, coriander, bay leaf, half of the fried tortilla strips, reserved peppers and, if desired, jalapenos. Bring to a boil. Reduce heat; simmer, uncovered, 35 minutes.

5. Remove soup from heat; cool slightly. Discard bay leaf. Process in batches in a blender until blended. Return to the Dutch oven.

6. In the skillet, heat remaining oil over medium-high heat. Add chicken; cook and stir 4-5 minutes or until no longer pink. Add chicken, lemon juice, salt, pepper and cayenne to the soup; heat through. Serve with cheese, avocado and tortilla strips.

NOTE *Wear disposable gloves when cutting hot peppers; the oils can burn skin. Avoid touching your face.*

CHEESY BROCCOLI SOUP

PREP: 15 MIN. • **COOK:** 3 HOURS • **MAKES:** 4 SERVINGS

- 2 **tablespoons butter**
- 1 **small onion, finely chopped**
- 2 **cups finely chopped fresh broccoli**
- 3 **cups reduced-sodium chicken broth**
- 1 **can (12 ounces) evaporated milk**
- ½ **teaspoon pepper**
- 1 **package (8 ounces) process cheese (Velveeta), cubed**
- 1½ **cups shredded extra-sharp cheddar cheese**
- 1 **cup shredded Parmesan cheese**
  Additional shredded extra-sharp cheddar cheese

1. In a small skillet, heat butter over medium-high heat. Add onion; cook and stir 3-4 minutes or until tender. Transfer to a 3- or 4-qt. slow cooker. Add broccoli, broth, milk and pepper.
2. Cook, covered, on low for 3-4 hours or until broccoli is tender. Stir in process cheese until melted. Add shredded cheeses; stir until melted. Just before serving, stir soup to combine. Top servings with additional cheddar cheese.

Whenever I order soup at a restaurant, I go for broccoli-cheese. I finally put my slow cooker to the test and made my own. It took a few tries, but now my soup is exactly how I like it.

—**KRISTEN HILLS** LAYTON, UT

VEGETABLE SOUP

If the cold winter weather is getting you down, warm up Southern-style with a pot of this veggie soup.
—**CHRISTY HINRICHS** PARKVILLE, MO

START TO FINISH: 30 MIN. • **MAKES:** 6 SERVINGS (2½ QUARTS)

- ½ **cup chopped onion**
- 2 **teaspoons olive oil**
- 2 **teaspoons minced garlic**
- 2 **cans (14½ ounces each) vegetable broth**
- 1 **can (28 ounces) crushed tomatoes**
- 1 **package (16 ounces) frozen mixed vegetables**
- 1 **cup sliced fresh or frozen okra**
- 1 **can (4 ounces) chopped green chilies**
- 2 **teaspoons dried savory**
- 1 **teaspoon sugar**
- ½ **teaspoon salt**
- ½ **teaspoon dried tarragon**
- ⅛ **teaspoon white pepper**

1. In a Dutch oven over medium-high heat, saute onion in oil for 3 minutes or until tender. Add garlic; cook 1 minute longer. Stir in the remaining ingredients. Bring to a boil over medium-high heat. Reduce heat; cover and simmer for 15-20 minutes or until vegetables are crisp-tender.

2. Serve immediately or transfer to freezer containers. May be frozen for up to 3 months.

TO USE FROZEN SOUP *Thaw soup in the refrigerator overnight. Transfer to a saucepan. Cover and cook over medium heat until heated through.*

THE BEST CHICKEN & DUMPLINGS

Chicken and dumplings harken back to the nippy days of my childhood.

—ERIKA MONROE-WILLIAMS
SCOTTSDALE, AZ

PREP: 25 MIN. • **COOK:** 1 HOUR 10 MIN.
MAKES: 8 SERVINGS (3 QUARTS)

- ¾ **cup all-purpose flour, divided**
- ½ **teaspoon salt**
- ½ **teaspoon freshly ground pepper**
- 1 **broiler/fryer chicken (about 3 pounds), cut up**
- 2 **tablespoons canola oil**
- 1 **large onion, chopped**
- 2 **medium carrots, chopped**
- 2 **celery ribs, chopped**
- 3 **garlic cloves, minced**
- 6 **cups chicken stock**
- ½ **cup white wine or apple cider**
- 2 **teaspoons sugar**
- 2 **bay leaves**
- 5 **whole peppercorns**

DUMPLINGS
- 1⅓ **cups all-purpose flour**
- 2 **teaspoons baking powder**
- ¾ **teaspoon salt**
- ⅔ **cup 2% milk**
- 1 **tablespoon butter, melted**

ASSEMBLY
- ½ **cup heavy whipping cream**
- 2 **teaspoons minced fresh parsley**
- 2 **teaspoons minced fresh thyme**
  Salt and pepper to taste

1. In a shallow bowl, mix ½ cup flour, salt and pepper. Add chicken and toss to coat; shake off excess. In a 6-qt. stockpot, heat oil over medium-high heat. Brown the chicken on all sides; remove from pan.

2. Add onion, carrots and celery to the same pan; cook and stir for 6-8 minutes or until the onion is tender. Add garlic; cook and stir 1 minute longer. Stir in ¼ cup flour until blended. Gradually add stock, stirring constantly. Stir in wine, sugar, bay leaves and peppercorns. Return chicken to pan; bring to a boil. Reduce heat; simmer, covered, 20-25 minutes or until chicken juices run clear.

3. Meanwhile, in a bowl, whisk flour, baking powder and salt. In another bowl, whisk milk and melted butter until blended. Add to flour mixture; stir just until moistened (do not overmix). Drop by rounded tablespoons onto a parchment paper-lined baking sheet; set aside.

4. Remove chicken from stockpot; cool slightly. Discard bay leaves and skim fat from soup. Remove skin and bones from chicken and discard. Using two forks, coarsely shred meat into 1- to 1½-in. pieces; return to soup. Cook, covered, on high until mixture reaches a simmer.

5. Drop dumplings on top of the simmering soup. Reduce heat to low; cook, covered, 15-18 minutes or until a toothpick inserted in the center of the dumplings comes out clean (do not lift cover while simmering). Gently stir in cream, parsley and thyme. Season with additional salt and pepper to taste.

ULTIMATE BEEF CHILI

PREP: 15 MIN. • **COOK:** 35 MIN.
MAKES: 6 SERVINGS

- 1 pound lean ground beef (90% lean)
- 1 small green pepper, chopped
- 1 small onion, chopped
- 1 can (15 ounces) Ranch Style beans (pinto beans in seasoned tomato sauce)
- 2 cans (14½ ounces each) no-salt-added diced tomatoes, undrained
- 4 teaspoons chili powder
- 1¼ teaspoons ground cumin
- ½ teaspoon pepper
- 6 small wedges of blue cheese, optional

1. In a large saucepan, cook the beef, green pepper and onion over medium heat until the meat is no longer pink; drain.
2. Stir in the beans, tomatoes, chili powder, cumin and pepper. Bring to a boil. Reduce heat; cover and simmer for 15 minutes or until flavors are blended. Top with cheese if desired.

> Blue cheese is an unusual ingredient to add to chili, but it adds a creamy, punchy accent. People will be asking you for the secret ingredient.
>
> **—LUANN MANER CROSBY** TAYLOR, AZ

NOTES

SHRIMP EGG DROP SOUP

Who knew that egg drop soup could be so easy? It's only three simple steps to this better-than-restaurant-quality soup with just the right blend of veggies and shrimp.
—*TASTE OF HOME* TEST KITCHEN

START TO FINISH: 30 MIN. • **MAKES:** 4 SERVINGS

- 4 **teaspoons cornstarch**
- ½ **teaspoon soy sauce**
- ⅛ **teaspoon ground ginger**
- 1½ **cups cold water, divided**
- 2 **cans (14½ ounces each) chicken broth**
- 1½ **cups frozen home-style egg noodles**
- 1 **cup frozen broccoli florets, thawed and coarsely chopped**
- ½ **cup julienned carrot**
- 1 **large egg, lightly beaten**
- ½ **pound cooked medium shrimp, peeled and deveined**

1. In a small bowl, combine the cornstarch, soy sauce, ginger and ½ cup cold water; set aside.

2. In a large saucepan, combine broth and the remaining water. Bring to a simmer; add noodles. Cook, uncovered, for 15 minutes. Add broccoli and carrot; simmer 3-4 minutes longer or until noodles are tender.

3. Drizzle beaten egg into hot soup, stirring constantly. Stir cornstarch mixture and add to the pan. Bring to a boil; cook and stir for 2 minutes or until slightly thickened. Add cooked shrimp; heat through.

TOMATO SOUP WITH TORTELLINI

Tortellini gives stick-to-your-ribs goodness to this garden-fresh tomato soup. It's a staple at our house.
—**SUSAN PECK** REPUBLIC, MO

PREP: 20 MIN. • **COOK:** 40 MIN. • **MAKES:** 8 SERVINGS (2 QUARTS)

- 1 **large onion, chopped**
- 1 **tablespoon butter**
- 2 **pounds plum tomatoes, seeded and quartered**
- 3 **cups reduced-sodium chicken broth or vegetable broth**
- 1 **can (8 ounces) tomato sauce**
- 1 **tablespoon minced fresh basil**
- ¼ **teaspoon salt**
  Dash pepper
- 1 **cup dried cheese tortellini**
- ⅓ **cup shredded Parmesan cheese**

1. In a large saucepan, saute onion in butter until tender. Add the tomatoes, broth, tomato sauce, basil, salt and pepper. Bring to a boil. Reduce heat; cover and simmer for 30 minutes. Cool slightly.

2. Cook the tortellini according to package directions; drain well and set aside. In a blender, cover and process soup in batches until smooth. Return to the saucepan; add the tortellini and heat through. Garnish with cheese.

NOTES

COLORFUL MINESTRONE

A rainbow of vegetables are featured in this vegetarian soup. You can use any multi-colored pasta in place of the rotini.

—CRYSTAL SCHLUETER NORTHGLENN, CO

PREP: 20 MIN. • **COOK:** 6 HOURS 20 MIN.
MAKES: 10 SERVINGS (3¾ QUARTS)

4	stalks Swiss chard (about ½ pound)
2	tablespoons olive oil
1	medium red onion, finely chopped
6	cups vegetable broth
2	cans (14½ ounces each) fire-roasted diced tomatoes, undrained
1	can (16 ounces) kidney beans, rinsed and drained
1	can (15 ounces) chickpeas, rinsed and drained
1	medium yellow summer squash or zucchini, halved and cut into ¼-inch slices
1	medium sweet red or yellow pepper, finely chopped
1	medium carrot, finely chopped
2	garlic cloves, minced
1½	cups uncooked spiral pasta
¼	cup prepared pesto

1. Cut stems from chard; chop stems and leaves separately. Reserve leaves for adding later. In a large skillet, heat oil over medium heat. Add onion and chard stems; cook and stir for 3-5 minutes or until tender. Transfer to a 6-qt. slow cooker.
2. Stir in broth, tomatoes, beans, chickpeas, squash, pepper, carrot and garlic. Cook, covered, on low for 6-8 hours or until the vegetables are tender.
3. Stir in pasta and reserved chard leaves. Cook, covered, on low 20-25 minutes longer or until pasta is tender. Top individual servings with pesto.

FRENCH ONION SOUP

I top this rich soup with Brie, prosciutto and garlic on French bread to make it extra appealing.

—LAURA MCALLISTER
MORGANTON, NC

PREP: 1½ HOURS • **BAKE:** 10 MIN.
MAKES: 9 SERVINGS

- ¼ **cup butter, cubed**
- ¼ **cup plus 1 tablespoon olive oil, divided**
- 6 **large sweet onions, thinly sliced (about 12 cups)**
- 1 **whole garlic bulb**
- ¼ **cup dry red wine or beef broth**
- 6 **cups beef broth**
- 1½ **teaspoons Worcestershire sauce**
- 1 **bay leaf**
  Dash cayenne pepper
  Pepper to taste
- 9 **slices French bread (1 inch thick)**
- 1 **round (8 ounces) Brie cheese, rind removed, softened**
- 6 **thin slices prosciutto or deli ham, chopped**
- 2 **cups grated Parmesan cheese**

1. In Dutch oven over medium heat, melt butter with ¼ cup oil; add onions. Cook, stirring occasionally, for 15 minutes. Reduce heat to low. Cook 45 minutes longer or until the onions are golden, stirring occasionally.

2. Meanwhile, remove papery outer skin from garlic (do not peel or separate cloves). Cut top off the garlic bulb; brush with remaining oil. Wrap in heavy-duty foil.

3. Bake the garlic at 425° for 30-35 minutes or until softened. Cool for 10-15 minutes. Squeeze softened garlic into a small bowl; mash and set aside.

4. Add wine to the onion mixture; cook for 2 minutes. Stir in broth, Worcestershire sauce, bay leaf, cayenne and pepper. Bring to a boil. Reduce heat; simmer, uncovered, for 15-20 minutes.

5. Place bread slices on a baking sheet. Bake at 425° for 3-5 minutes or until golden brown, turning once. Spread each slice with Brie and mashed garlic; sprinkle with prosciutto.

6. Discard the bay leaf from the soup; ladle 1 cup into each of nine ovenproof bowls. Top each with one slice of toast; sprinkle with Parmesan cheese. Place bowls on a baking sheet. Bake for 10 minutes or until cheese is melted.

NEW ENGLAND CLAM CHOWDER

In the Pacific Northwest, we dig our own razor clams and grind them for the chowder. Since those aren't readily available elsewhere, canned clams are acceptable.

—SANDY LARSON PORT ANGELES, WA

PREP: 20 MIN. • **COOK:** 35 MIN. • **MAKES:** 5 SERVINGS

- 4 **center-cut bacon strips**
- 2 **celery ribs, chopped**
- 1 **large onion, chopped**
- 1 **garlic clove, minced**
- 3 **small potatoes, peeled and cubed**
- 1 **cup water**
- 1 **bottle (8 ounces) clam juice**
- 3 **teaspoons reduced-sodium chicken bouillon granules**
- ¼ **teaspoon white pepper**
- ¼ **teaspoon dried thyme**
- ⅓ **cup all-purpose flour**
- 2 **cups fat-free half-and-half, divided**
- 2 **cans (6½ ounces each) chopped clams, undrained**

1. In a Dutch oven, cook bacon over medium heat until crisp. Remove to paper towels to drain; set aside. Saute celery and onion in the drippings until tender. Add garlic; cook 1 minute longer. Stir in the potatoes, water, clam juice, bouillon, pepper and thyme. Bring to a boil. Reduce heat; simmer, uncovered, for 15-20 minutes or until potatoes are tender.

2. In a small bowl, combine flour and 1 cup half-and-half until smooth. Gradually stir into soup. Bring to a boil; cook and stir for 1-2 minutes or until thickened.

3. Stir in clams and the remaining half-and-half; heat through (do not boil). Crumble the cooked bacon; sprinkle over each serving.

BEANS, PASTA & **MORE**

SPICY LENTIL SOUP

I've finally found a lentil soup my husband enjoys! Adjust the spice level to your taste, and present this yummy soup with warm pita bread.

—EVA BARKER LEBANON, NH

PREP: 25 MIN. • **COOK:** 9 HOURS
MAKES: 14 SERVINGS (3½ QUARTS)

- 1½ **pounds potatoes, peeled and cubed (about 5 cups)**
- 1 **large onion, chopped**
- 2 **large carrots, chopped**
- 2 **celery ribs, chopped**
- ¼ **cup olive oil**
- 4 **teaspoons ground cumin**
- 2 **teaspoons chili powder**
- 1 **teaspoon salt**
- 1 **teaspoon ground coriander**
- 1 **teaspoon coarsely ground pepper**
- ½ **teaspoon ground turmeric**
- ½ **teaspoon cayenne pepper**
- 5 **garlic cloves, minced**
- 2 **cartons (32 ounces each) reduced-sodium chicken broth**
- 2 **cans (15 ounces each) tomato sauce**
- 1 **package (16 ounces) dried lentils, rinsed**
- ¼ **cup lemon juice**

1. Place potatoes, onion, carrots and celery in a 6-qt. slow cooker. In a small skillet, heat oil over medium heat. Add seasonings; cook and stir 2 minutes. Add garlic; cook 1-2 minutes longer. Transfer to the slow cooker.

2. Stir in broth, tomato sauce and lentils. Cook, covered, on low for 9-11 hours or until lentils are tender. Stir in lemon juice.

NOTES

BLOODY MARY SOUP WITH BEANS

A good Bloody Mary inspired this soup. It packs a punch to warm you up on a chilly day. For a meat-free meal, substitute veggie broth.
—**AMBER MASSEY** ARGYLE, TX

PREP: 20 MIN. • **COOK:** 55 MIN. • **MAKES:** 16 SERVINGS (4 QUARTS)

- 1 **tablespoon olive oil**
- 1 **large onion, chopped**
- 2 **celery ribs, chopped**
- 1 **large carrot, finely chopped**
- 1 **poblano pepper, seeded and chopped**
- 3 **garlic cloves, minced**
- 1 **carton (32 ounces) reduced-sodium chicken broth**
- 1 **can (28 ounces) crushed tomatoes**
- 1 **can (14½ ounces) fire-roasted diced tomatoes, undrained**
- ¼ **cup tomato paste**
- 2 **cans (15 ounces each) white kidney or cannellini beans, rinsed and drained**
- ¼ **cup vodka**
- 2 **tablespoons Worcestershire sauce**
- ½ **teaspoon sugar**
- 2 **tablespoons lemon juice**
- 1 **tablespoon prepared horseradish**
- ½ **teaspoon pepper**
  Minced fresh parsley, celery ribs, lemon wedges and hot pepper sauce, optional

1. In a Dutch oven, heat oil over medium-high heat. Add onion, celery, carrot and pepper; cook and stir 4-5 minutes or until crisp-tender. Add garlic; cook 1 minute longer.

2. Stir in broth, tomatoes and tomato paste. Bring to a boil. Reduce heat; simmer, covered, for 15 minutes. Add beans, vodka, Worcestershire sauce and sugar; return to a boil. Reduce heat; simmer, uncovered, 25-30 minutes or until vegetables are tender, stirring occasionally.

3. Stir in lemon juice, horseradish and pepper. Garnish servings with optional ingredients as desired.

NOTE *Wear disposable gloves when cutting hot peppers; the oils can burn skin. Avoid touching your face.*

GINGER CHICKEN NOODLE SOUP

PREP: 15 MIN. • **COOK:** 3½ HOURS
MAKES: 8 SERVINGS (2½ QUARTS)

- 1 **pound boneless skinless chicken breasts, cubed**
- 2 **medium carrots, shredded**
- 3 **tablespoons sherry or reduced-sodium chicken broth**
- 2 **tablespoons rice vinegar**
- 1 **tablespoon reduced-sodium soy sauce**
- 2 **to 3 teaspoons minced fresh gingerroot**
- ¼ **teaspoon pepper**
- 6 **cups reduced-sodium chicken broth**
- 1 **cup water**
- 2 **cups fresh snow peas, halved**
- 2 **ounces uncooked angel hair pasta, broken into thirds**

1. In a 5-qt. slow cooker, combine the first seven ingredients; stir in broth and water. Cook, covered, on low for 3-4 hours or until the chicken is tender.

2. Stir in snow peas and pasta. Cook, covered, on low for 30 minutes longer or until snow peas and pasta are tender.

This is one of my favorite soup recipes to serve in the wintertime because it's super easy to make and fills the whole house with a wonderful aroma. My entire family loves it!

—BRANDY STANSBURY EDNA, TX

BEAN & BUTTERNUT SOUP

The delicious combination of squash, sausage, beans and veggies makes this my go-to soup in fall. It's full of freshness.
—**JAYE BEELER** GRAND RAPIDS, MI

PREP: 20 MIN. • **COOK:** 40 MIN.
MAKES: 12 SERVINGS (4½ QUARTS)

- 1 **pound bulk Italian sausage**
- 1 **medium onion, chopped**
- 1 **medium sweet red pepper, chopped**
- 4 **garlic cloves, minced**
- 1 **large butternut squash (about 5 pounds), peeled, seeded and cut into 1-inch pieces**
- 1 **package (16 ounces) frozen corn, divided**
- 4 **cups water**
- 1 **tablespoon chicken base**
- 2 **cans (15½ ounces each) great northern beans, rinsed and drained**
- 2 **cans (14½ ounces each) fire-roasted diced tomatoes, undrained**
- 1 **teaspoon salt**
- ¼ **teaspoon pepper**
  Heavy whipping cream and fresh parsley, optional

1. In a stockpot, cook sausage, onion and red pepper over medium heat for 9-11 minutes or until the sausage is no longer pink and the onion is tender, breaking sausage into crumbles. Add garlic; cook for 1 minute longer. Remove with a slotted spoon; discard drippings.

2. Add squash, 1½ cups corn, water and chicken base to the same pot; bring to a boil. Reduce heat; simmer, covered, 15-20 minutes or until the squash is tender.

3. Remove soup from heat; cool slightly. Process in batches in a blender until smooth. Return to pot. Add the beans, tomatoes, salt, pepper, sausage mixture and remaining corn; heat through. Top servings with cream and minced parsley.

FREEZE OPTION *Freeze cooled soup in freezer containers. To use, partially thaw in refrigerator overnight. Heat through in a saucepan, stirring occasionally and adding a little water if necessary.*

HELPFUL HINT

When a *Taste of Home* recipe calls for Italian sausage, it is referring to sweet Italian sausage. Recipes using hot Italian sausage specifically call for that type of sausage.

SPICY BARLEY & LENTIL SOUP

PREP: 15 MIN. • **COOK:** 55 MIN.
MAKES: 12 SERVINGS (4½ QUARTS)

- 1 **tablespoon olive oil**
- 1 **package (14 ounces) smoked kielbasa or Polish sausage, halved lengthwise and sliced**
- 4 **medium carrots, chopped**
- 1 **medium onion, chopped**
- 2 **garlic cloves, minced**
- ¾ **teaspoon ground cumin**
- 1 **can (28 ounces) crushed tomatoes**
- 1 **package (16 ounces) dried lentils, rinsed**
- 1 **can (15 ounces) black beans, rinsed and drained**
- ¾ **cup medium pearl barley**
- ½ **cup frozen corn**
- 10 **cups reduced-sodium chicken broth**

1. In a 6-qt. stockpot, heat oil over medium heat. Add the kielbasa; cook and stir for 6-8 minutes or until browned. Remove from pan with a slotted spoon.

2. Add carrots and onion to the same pot; cook and stir for 6-8 minutes or until tender. Add garlic and cumin; cook 1 minute longer. Stir in kielbasa and remaining ingredients; bring to a boil. Reduce heat; simmer, covered, 35-45 minutes or until lentils and barley are tender, stirring occasionally.

> My family has been making lentil soup every New Year's since I was little. We have tweaked it over time, and now all our family and friends love it.
>
> —**KRISTEN HEIGL** STATEN ISLAND, NY

OLD-FASHIONED TURKEY NOODLE SOUP

Make the most of leftover turkey with this delicious homemade soup. Roasting the turkey bones, garlic and vegetables adds a rich flavor without added fat.

—TASTE OF HOME TEST KITCHEN

PREP: 4 HOURS + CHILLING
COOK: 45 MIN. • **MAKES:** 10 SERVINGS (ABOUT 4 QUARTS)

BROTH

- 1 **leftover turkey carcass (from a 12- to 14-pound turkey)**
- 2 **cooked turkey wings, meat removed**
- 2 **cooked turkey drumsticks, meat removed**
- 1 **turkey neck bone**
- 1 **medium unpeeled onion, cut into wedges**
- 2 **small unpeeled carrots, cut into chunks**
- 6 **to 8 garlic cloves, peeled**
- 4 **quarts plus 1 cup cold water, divided**

SOUP

- 3 **quarts water**
- 5 **cups uncooked egg noodles**
- 2 **cups diced carrots**
- 2 **cups diced celery**
- 3 **cups cubed cooked turkey**
- ¼ **cup minced fresh parsley**
- 2½ **teaspoons salt**
- 2 **teaspoons dried thyme**
- 1 **teaspoon pepper**

1. Place the turkey carcass, bones from wings and drumsticks, neck bone, onion, carrots and garlic in a 15x10x1-in. baking pan coated with cooking spray. Bake, uncovered, at 400° for 1 hour, turning once.

2. Transfer the carcass, bones and vegetables to an 8-qt. stockpot. Add 4 qts. cold water; set aside. Pour remaining cold water into the baking pan, stirring to loosen the browned bits. Add to pot. Bring to a boil. Reduce heat; cover and simmer for 3-4 hours.

3. Cool slightly. Strain broth; discard bones and vegetables. Set stockpot in an ice-water bath until the broth cools, stirring occasionally. Cover and refrigerate overnight.

4. Skim fat from the broth. Cover and bring to a boil. Reduce heat to a simmer. Meanwhile, in a Dutch oven, bring 3 qts. water to a boil. Add noodles and carrots; cook for 4 minutes. Add celery; cook 5-7 minutes longer or until noodles and vegetables are tender. Drain; add to simmering broth. Add cubed turkey; heat through. Stir in the parsley, salt, thyme and pepper.

SPICY SWEET POTATO KALE SOUP

This cross between a soup and a stew fits the meatless Monday bill quite nicely. It warms you right up, and satisfies without leaving you overstuffed.

—MARYBETH MANK MESQUITE, TX

PREP: 25 MIN. • **COOK:** 40 MIN.
MAKES: 12 SERVINGS (3 QUARTS)

- 2 tablespoons olive oil
- 1 medium onion, finely chopped
- 3 garlic cloves, minced
- 3 pounds sweet potatoes (about 5 medium), cubed
- 2 medium Granny Smith apples, peeled and chopped
- 1 teaspoon honey
- 1 teaspoon rubbed sage
- ¾ to 1 teaspoon crushed red pepper flakes
- ½ teaspoon salt
- ¼ teaspoon pepper
- 3 cans (14½ ounces each) vegetable broth
- 2 cans (15 ounces each) cannellini or white kidney beans, rinsed and drained
- 3 cups chopped fresh kale
- ½ cup heavy whipping cream
  Optional toppings: olive oil, giardiniera and shredded Parmesan cheese

1. In a 6-qt. stockpot, heat oil over medium-high heat. Add onion; cook and stir 6-8 minutes or until tender. Add garlic; cook 1 minute longer. Stir in sweet potatoes, apples, honey, seasonings and broth. Bring to a boil. Reduce heat; simmer, covered, for 25-30 minutes or until the potatoes are tender.

2. Puree soup using an immersion blender. Or, cool soup slightly and puree in batches in a blender; return to pan. Add beans and kale; cook, uncovered, over medium heat 10-15 minutes or until kale is tender, stirring occasionally. Stir in cream. Serve with toppings as desired.

WHITE BEAN & CHICKEN ENCHILADA SOUP

I made this soup to please my daughters' craving for creaminess, my husband's for spice and mine for white beans. Garnish with jalapenos, sour cream and green onions.
—**DARCY GONZALEZ** PALMDALE, CA

PREP: 15 MIN. • **COOK:** 20 MIN.
MAKES: 8 SERVINGS

- 4 cans (15½ ounces each) great northern beans, rinsed and drained
- 3 boneless skinless chicken breasts (6 ounces each), cubed
- ½ medium onion, chopped
- 1 garlic clove, minced
- 2 cups frozen corn, thawed
- 1 can (10¾ ounces) condensed cream of chicken soup, undiluted
- 1 carton (32 ounces) reduced-sodium chicken broth
- 1 tablespoon ground cumin
- 2 seeded and chopped jalapeno peppers, divided
- 1 teaspoon pepper
- 2 green onions, chopped
  Sour cream, shredded cheddar cheese and tortilla chips
  Fresh cilantro leaves, optional

1. In a large stockpot, combine the first eight ingredients. Add 1 chopped jalapeno and ground pepper. Bring to a boil. Reduce heat; simmer, covered, until the chicken is no longer pink and soup is heated through, 15-20 minutes.

2. Serve with the remaining chopped jalapeno; top each serving with green onions, sour cream, cheese and tortilla chips. If desired, add cilantro leaves.

HERBED CHICKEN & SPINACH SOUP

PREP: 20 MIN. • **COOK:** 4½ HOURS • **MAKES:** 4 SERVINGS

- 1 **pound boneless skinless chicken thighs, cut into ½-inch pieces**
- 1 **can (16 ounces) kidney beans, rinsed and drained**
- 1 **can (14½ ounces) chicken broth**
- 1 **medium onion, chopped**
- 1 **medium sweet red pepper, chopped**
- 1 **celery rib, chopped**
- 2 **tablespoons tomato paste**
- 3 **garlic cloves, minced**
- ½ **teaspoon minced fresh rosemary or ¼ teaspoon dried rosemary, crushed**
- ½ **teaspoon minced fresh thyme or ¼ teaspoon dried thyme**
- ½ **teaspoon dried oregano**
- ¼ **teaspoon salt**
- ¼ **teaspoon pepper**
- 3 **cups fresh baby spinach**
- ¼ **cup shredded Parmesan cheese**

In a 3-qt. slow cooker, combine the first 13 ingredients. Cover and cook on low for 4-5 hours or until the chicken is tender. Stir in spinach; cook 30 minutes longer or until the spinach is wilted. Top with cheese.

To create a hearty meal, I serve this substantial chicken soup with a side of crusty bread slathered in butter.

—**TANYA MACDONALD** ANTIGONISH COUNTY, NS

WINTER COUNTRY SOUP

My soup will warm your family up on the chilliest of winter nights! Featuring smoked sausage, beans and vegetables, it's a hearty way to start a meal or a satisfying lunch all by itself.

—JEANNETTE SABO LEXINGTON PARK, MD

PREP: 15 MIN. • **COOK:** 40 MIN.
MAKES: 12 SERVINGS (3 QUARTS)

- 1 **package (14 ounces) smoked sausage, cut into ¼-inch slices**
- 1 **large sweet red pepper, cut into ½-inch pieces**
- 8 **shallots, chopped**
- 1 **tablespoon butter**
- 8 **cups chopped fresh kale**
- 8 **cups vegetable broth**
- 3 **cups frozen corn**
- 1 **can (15½ ounces) great northern beans, rinsed and drained**
- ½ **teaspoon cayenne pepper**
- ¼ **teaspoon pepper**
- ¾ **cup uncooked orzo pasta**

1. In a Dutch oven, saute the sausage, red pepper and shallots in butter until the vegetables are tender.

2. Add kale; cover and cook for 2-3 minutes or until kale is wilted. Stir in the broth, corn, beans, cayenne and pepper. Bring to a boil. Reduce heat; simmer, uncovered, for 20 minutes. Return to a boil. Stir in orzo. Cook 8-10 minutes longer or until the pasta is tender.

SLOW COOKER PORK POZOLE

When the snow begins to fall, I prepare a heartwarming stew with pork ribs and hominy. This recipe makes a fill-you-up bowl of lightly spiced comfort. Yum!

—GENIE GUNN ASHEVILLE, NC

PREP: 10 MIN. • **COOK:** 3 HOURS
MAKES: 6 SERVINGS

- 1 **can (15½ ounces) hominy, rinsed and drained**
- 1 **can (14½ ounces) diced tomatoes, undrained**
- 1 **can (14½ ounces) diced tomatoes with mild green chilies, undrained**
- 1 **can (10 ounces) green enchilada sauce**
- 2 **medium carrots, finely chopped**
- 1 **medium onion, finely chopped**
- 3 **garlic cloves, minced**
- 2 **teaspoons ground cumin**
- ¼ **teaspoon salt**
- 1 **pound boneless country-style pork ribs**
  Lime wedges and minced fresh cilantro
  Corn tortillas, optional

1. In a 3- or 4-qt. slow cooker, combine the first nine ingredients; add pork. Cook, covered, on low for 3-4 hours or until the pork is tender.

2. Remove the pork from slow cooker. Cut into bite-size pieces; return to slow cooker. Serve with lime wedges and cilantro and, if desired, corn tortillas.

NOTES

ITALIAN WHITE BEAN SOUP

A bowlful of this soup is so satisfying! With lots of filling beans, potatoes and other veggies, it's a vegetarian recipe that even hits the spot with meat lovers.
—**KRISTINA KRUMMEL** ELKINS, AR

START TO FINISH: 30 MIN. • **MAKES:** 6 SERVINGS

- 1 tablespoon olive oil
- 1 medium potato, peeled and cut into ½-inch cubes
- 2 medium carrots, chopped
- 1 medium onion, chopped
- 2 celery ribs, chopped
- 1 medium zucchini, chopped
- 1 teaspoon finely chopped seeded jalapeno pepper
- 1 can (15½ ounces) navy beans, rinsed and drained
- 2 to 2½ cups vegetable or chicken broth
- 1 can (8 ounces) tomato sauce
- 2 tablespoons minced fresh parsley or 2 teaspoons dried parsley flakes
- 1½ teaspoons minced fresh thyme or ½ teaspoon dried thyme

1. In a Dutch oven, heat oil over medium-high heat. Add potato and carrots; cook and stir for 3 minutes. Add onion, celery, zucchini and jalapeno; cook and stir for 3-4 minutes or until the vegetables are crisp-tender.

2. Stir in the remaining ingredients; bring to a boil. Reduce heat; simmer, covered, 12-15 minutes or until the vegetables are tender.

FREEZE OPTION *Freeze cooled soup in freezer containers. To use, partially thaw in refrigerator overnight. Heat through in a saucepan, stirring occasionally and adding a little broth or water if necessary.*

NOTE *Wear disposable gloves when cutting hot peppers; the oils can burn skin. Avoid touching your face.*

HELPFUL HINT

To get the most flavor from dried herbs, I put the desired amount in the palm of my hand, then rub my hands together over the pot, letting the herbs fall into the dish. This releases the oils in the herbs.

—**BRAD H.,** TEMECULA, CA.

TORTELLINI & SPINACH SOUP

The first time I made this soup was in the summer, but when I saw its bright red and green colors, I thought that it would make a perfect first course for Christmas dinner as well.
—**MARIETTA SLATER** JUSTIN, TX

START TO FINISH: 25 MIN. • **MAKES:** 6 SERVINGS

- 2 cans (14½ ounces each) vegetable broth
- 1 package (9 ounces) refrigerated cheese tortellini or tortellini of your choice
- 1 can (15 ounces) white kidney or cannellini beans, rinsed and drained
- 1 can (14½ ounces) Italian diced tomatoes, undrained
- ¼ teaspoon salt
- ⅛ teaspoon pepper
- 3 cups fresh baby spinach
- 3 tablespoons minced fresh basil
- ¼ cup shredded Asiago cheese

1. In a large saucepan, bring broth to a boil. Add tortellini; reduce heat. Simmer, uncovered, for 5 minutes. Stir in the beans, tomatoes, salt and pepper; return to a simmer. Cook 4-5 minutes longer or until the tortellini are tender.

2. Stir in spinach and basil; cook until the spinach is wilted. Top individual servings with cheese.

NOTES

_____
_____
_____
_____
_____
_____
_____

SOUTHWEST MEATBALL SOUP

I turned leftover hamburgers into meatballs and dreamed up this cozy Southwestern soup. Now my Italian family asks for it over traditional wedding soup.
—**TEENA PETRUS** JOHNSTOWN, PA

START TO FINISH: 30 MIN. • **MAKES:** 6 SERVINGS

- 1 **tablespoon canola oil**
- 2 **medium carrots, chopped**
- 2 **medium celery ribs, chopped**
- ½ **cup frozen corn, thawed**
- 2 **quarts chicken stock**
- 1 **cup soft bread crumbs**
- 1 **envelope reduced-sodium taco seasoning**
- 1 **large egg**
- 1 **pound ground chicken**
- 1½ **cups acini di pepe pasta**
- 2 **tablespoons minced fresh cilantro**
- ¼ **teaspoon salt**
  Cubed avocado and sour cream

1. In a Dutch oven, heat oil over medium heat. Add carrots, celery and corn; cook until tender. Stir in stock. Increase heat to high; bring to a boil.

2. Meanwhile, combine bread crumbs, taco seasoning, egg and chicken; mix lightly. With wet hands, shape into 1½-in. balls. Reduce heat to simmer; gently drop the meatballs into stock. Cook, covered, until the meatballs are no longer pink, 8-10 minutes. Stir in pasta. Simmer, covered, until the pasta is tender, 6-8 minutes. Sprinkle with cilantro and salt.

3. Serve with avocado and sour cream.

WHITE BEAN SOUP WITH ESCAROLE

This tomato-based soup has become a favorite because it uses kitchen staples, is packed with healthy ingredients and is a cinch to prepare. If I can't find escarole, I substitute fresh spinach at the very end of cooking.

—**GINA SAMOKAR** NORTH HAVEN, CT

PREP: 15 MIN. • **COOK:** 35 MIN. • **MAKES:** 8 SERVINGS (2 QUARTS)

- 1 **tablespoon olive oil**
- 1 **small onion, chopped**
- 5 **garlic cloves, minced**
- 3 **cans (14½ ounces each) reduced-sodium chicken broth**
- 1 **can (14½ ounces) diced tomatoes, undrained**
- ½ **teaspoon Italian seasoning**
- ¼ **teaspoon crushed red pepper flakes**
- 1 **cup uncooked whole wheat orzo pasta**
- 1 **bunch escarole or spinach, coarsely chopped (about 8 cups)**
- 1 **can (15 ounces) white kidney or cannellini beans, rinsed and drained**
- ¼ **cup grated Parmesan cheese**

1. In a Dutch oven, heat oil over medium heat. Add onion and garlic; cook and stir until tender. Add broth, tomatoes, Italian seasoning and pepper flakes; bring to a boil. Reduce heat; simmer, uncovered, for 15 minutes.

2. Stir in orzo and escarole. Return to a boil; cook for 12-14 minutes or until the orzo is tender. Add beans; heat through, stirring occasionally. Sprinkle servings with cheese.

FREEZE OPTION *Freeze cooled soup in freezer containers. To use, partially thaw in refrigerator overnight. Heat through in a saucepan, stirring occasionally and adding a little broth if necessary.*

LASAGNA SOUP

START TO FINISH: 30 MIN. • **MAKES:** 8 SERVINGS (2¾ QUARTS)

- 1 **pound lean ground beef (90% lean)**
- 1 **large green pepper, chopped**
- 1 **medium onion, chopped**
- 2 **garlic cloves, minced**
- 2 **cans (14½ ounces each) diced tomatoes, undrained**
- 2 **cans (14½ ounces each) reduced-sodium beef broth**
- 1 **can (8 ounces) tomato sauce**
- 1 **cup frozen corn**
- ¼ **cup tomato paste**
- 2 **teaspoons Italian seasoning**
- ¼ **teaspoon pepper**
- 2½ **cups uncooked spiral pasta**
- ½ **cup shredded Parmesan cheese**

1. In a large saucepan, cook beef, green pepper and onion over medium heat for 6-8 minutes or until the meat is no longer pink, breaking up beef into crumbles. Add garlic; cook 1 minute longer. Drain.

2. Stir in tomatoes, broth, tomato sauce, corn, tomato paste, Italian seasoning and pepper. Bring to a boil. Stir in pasta. Return to a boil. Reduce heat; simmer, covered, for 10-12 minutes or until pasta is tender. Sprinkle with cheese.

> All the traditional flavors of lasagna come together in this comforting bowl of soup.
>
> —**SHERYL OLENICK** DEMAREST, NJ

LENTIL-VEGETABLE SOUP

My mother is diabetic, so I often prepare this dish for her. I wanted a soup that hit the spot on cool nights, so I paired the lentils with turkey bacon and a handful of spices.
—**NICOLE HOPPING** PINOLE, CA

PREP: 15 MIN. • **COOK:** 45 MIN. • **MAKES:** 6 SERVINGS

- 6 **bacon strips, chopped**
- 1 **pound red potatoes (about 3 medium), chopped**
- 2 **medium carrots, chopped**
- 1 **medium onion, chopped**
- 6 **garlic cloves, minced**
- ¾ **teaspoon ground cumin**
- ½ **teaspoon salt**
- ½ **teaspoon rubbed sage**
- ½ **teaspoon dried thyme**
- ¼ **teaspoon pepper**
- 1½ **cups dried lentils, rinsed**
- 4 **cups chicken stock**

1. In a large saucepan, cook bacon over medium heat until crisp, stirring occasionally. Remove with a slotted spoon; drain on paper towels. Discard drippings, reserving 1 tablespoon in the pan. Add potatoes, carrots and onion; cook and stir for 6-8 minutes or until the carrots and onion are tender. Add garlic and seasonings; cook 1 minute longer.
2. Add lentils and stock; bring to a boil. Reduce heat; simmer, covered, 30-35 minutes or until the lentils and potatoes are tender. Top each serving with bacon.

TURKEY & NOODLE TOMATO SOUP

Turn V8 juice, ramen and frozen veggies into a wonderful soup that really satisfies. I like to serve it with biscuits.

—JENNIFER BRIDGES LOS ANGELES, CA

START TO FINISH: 25 MIN. • **MAKES:** 6 SERVINGS (2 QUARTS)

- 1 **pound ground turkey**
- 1 **envelope reduced-sodium onion soup mix**
- 1 **package (3 ounces) beef ramen noodles**
- 1½ **teaspoons sugar**
- ¾ **teaspoon pepper**
- ¼ **teaspoon salt**
- 1 **bottle (46 ounces) reduced-sodium V8 juice**
- 1 **package (16 ounces) frozen mixed vegetables**

1. In a Dutch oven, cook turkey over medium heat for 6-8 minutes or until no longer pink, breaking into crumbles; drain. Stir in soup mix, 1½ teaspoons seasoning from the noodles, sugar, pepper and salt. Add V8 juice and vegetables; bring to a boil. Reduce heat; simmer, uncovered, 5 minutes.

2. Break noodles into small pieces; add to soup (discard the remaining seasoning or save for another use). Cook 3-5 minutes longer or until the noodles are tender, stirring occasionally.

FREEZE OPTION *Freeze cooled soup in freezer containers. To use, partially thaw in refrigerator overnight. Heat through in a saucepan, stirring occasionally and adding a little reduced-sodium broth or water if necessary.*

RAMEN BROCCOLI SOUP

START TO FINISH: 20 MIN.
MAKES: 7 SERVINGS

- 5 **cups water**
- 1 **package (16 ounces) frozen broccoli cuts**
- 2 **packages (3 ounces each) chicken ramen noodles**
- ¼ **teaspoon garlic powder**
- 3 **slices process American cheese, cut into strips**

1. In a large saucepan, bring water to a boil. Add broccoli; return to a boil. Reduce heat; cover and simmer for 3 minutes. Return to a boil. Break noodles into small pieces; add to water. Cook 3 minutes longer, stirring occasionally.

2. Remove from the heat. Add the garlic powder, cheese and the contents of the seasoning packets from the noodles; stir until the cheese is melted. Serve immediately.

Cheese and garlic powder are the secret to this tasty and heartwarming soup. Loaded with noodles, it hits the spot on cold winter days.

—**LUELLA DIRKS** EMELLE, AL

NOTES

RAVIOLI SOUP

We adore pasta, so I used it as the inspiration for this soup. The meaty tomato base pairs perfectly with the cheesy ravioli pillows.

—SHELLEY WAY CHEYENNE, WY

PREP: 20 MIN. • **COOK:** 45 MIN.
MAKES: 10 SERVINGS (2½ QUARTS)

- 1 **pound ground beef**
- 2 **cups water**
- 2 **cans (one 28 ounces, one 14½ ounces) crushed tomatoes**
- 1 **can (6 ounces) tomato paste**
- 1½ **cups chopped onions**
- ¼ **cup minced fresh parsley**
- 2 **garlic cloves, minced**
- ¾ **teaspoon dried basil**
- ½ **teaspoon sugar**
- ½ **teaspoon dried oregano**
- ½ **teaspoon onion salt**
- ½ **teaspoon salt**
- ¼ **teaspoon pepper**
- ¼ **teaspoon dried thyme**
- 1 **package (9 ounces) refrigerated cheese ravioli**
- ¼ **cup grated Parmesan cheese**
  Additional minced fresh parsley, optional

In a Dutch oven, cook beef over medium heat until it is no longer pink; drain. Add the water, tomatoes, tomato paste, onions, parsley, garlic, basil, sugar, oregano, onion salt, salt, pepper and thyme; bring to a boil. Reduce heat; cover and simmer for 30 minutes. Cook ravioli according to the package directions; drain. Add to the soup and heat through. Stir in the Parmesan cheese. Sprinkle with additional parsley if desired.

CREAM SOUPS, BISQUES & CHOWDERS

BACON-CHEESEBURGER CHOWDER

The taste of a good bacon cheeseburger is hard to beat until you try this chowder! It's hearty, convenient and family friendly.
—**KRISTIN STONE** LITTLE ELM, TX

PREP: 15 MIN. • **COOK:** 30 MIN.
MAKES: 6 SERVINGS

- 1 **pound ground beef**
- 1 **medium onion, chopped**
- 1 **medium sweet red pepper, chopped**
- 1 **garlic clove, minced**
- 3 **tablespoons all-purpose flour**
- 2½ **cups 2% milk**
- 1 **pound potatoes (about 2 medium), peeled and chopped**
- 1½ **cups water**
- 1 **tablespoon reduced-sodium beef bouillon granules**
- 12 **ounces process cheese (Velveeta), cubed (about 2¼ cups)**
- 3 **bacon strips, cooked and crumbled**

1. In a 6-qt. stockpot, cook beef, onion and pepper over medium heat 6-8 minutes or until the beef is no longer pink and the onion is tender, breaking up beef into crumbles; drain. Add garlic to the beef mixture; cook 1 minute longer. Stir in flour until blended.

2. Gradually stir in milk. Add potatoes, water and bouillon; bring to a boil. Reduce heat; simmer, covered, for 15-20 minutes or until the potatoes are tender.

3. Add cheese; stir until melted. Sprinkle individual servings with bacon.

GINGER BUTTERNUT SQUASH BISQUE

The couple who introduced me to my husband made this soup for us one freezing night. The best part is that it's vegetarian, and yet it's filling enough even for my husband.
—**CARA MCDONALD** WINTER PARK, CO

PREP: 25 MIN. • **BAKE:** 40 MIN. + COOLING • **MAKES:** 6 SERVINGS

- 1 **medium butternut squash (about 3 pounds)**
- 1 **tablespoon olive oil**
- 2 **medium carrots, finely chopped**
- 1 **medium onion, chopped**
- 2 **garlic cloves, minced**
- 2 **teaspoons minced fresh gingerroot**
- 2 **teaspoons curry powder**
- 1 **can (14½ ounces) vegetable broth**
- 1 **can (13⅔ ounces) coconut milk**
- 1 **teaspoon salt**
- ½ **teaspoon pepper**
- 2 **cups hot cooked brown rice**
- ¼ **cup flaked coconut, toasted**
- ¼ **cup salted peanuts, coarsely chopped**
- ¼ **cup minced fresh cilantro**

1. Preheat oven to 400°. Cut squash in half lengthwise; remove and discard seeds. Place the squash cut side down in a greased shallow roasting pan. Roast for 40-45 minutes or until tender. Cool slightly.

2. In a large saucepan, heat oil over medium heat. Add carrots and onion; cook and stir until tender. Add garlic, ginger and curry powder; cook and stir for 1 minute longer. Add broth; bring to a boil. Reduce heat; simmer, uncovered, for 10-12 minutes or until the carrots are tender.

3. Scoop pulp from squash; discard the skins. Add squash pulp, coconut milk, salt and pepper to carrot mixture; bring just to a boil, stirring occasionally. Remove from heat; cool slightly. Process in batches in a blender until smooth.

4. Return to pan; heat through. Top individual servings with rice, coconut, peanuts and cilantro.

NOTE *To toast coconut, spread in a dry skillet; cook and stir over low heat until lightly browned.*

HELPFUL HINT

Choose butternut squash that feel heavy for their size and have hard, deep-colored, blemish-free rinds. Winter squash can be stored in a dry, cool, well-ventilated place for up to 1 month.

CREAM OF CAULIFLOWER SOUP

Cauliflower is often last on the list of vegetables my family will eat, but they love this creamy, savory soup with tender leeks and shredded cheddar cheese.
—**KRISTIN RIMKUS** SNOHOMISH, WA

PREP: 20 MIN. • **COOK:** 45 MIN. • **MAKES:** 8 SERVINGS (2 QUARTS)

- 1 **tablespoon olive oil**
- 1½ **cups thinly sliced leeks (white portion only)**
- 1 **medium head cauliflower, broken into florets**
- 1 **tablespoon minced fresh thyme or 1 teaspoon dried thyme**
- 2 **garlic cloves, minced**
- 1 **teaspoon Worcestershire sauce**
- 1 **carton (32 ounces) vegetable broth**
- 1 **can (12 ounces) reduced-fat evaporated milk**
- 1 **cup shredded sharp cheddar cheese**
  Additional shredded sharp cheddar cheese and minced fresh thyme, optional

1. In a large saucepan, heat oil over medium heat. Add leeks; cook and stir for 3-5 minutes or until tender. Stir in cauliflower, thyme, garlic and Worcestershire sauce. Add broth; bring to a boil. Reduce heat; simmer, covered, for 30-35 minutes or until the vegetables are very tender.

2. Puree soup using an immersion blender. Or, cool soup slightly and puree in batches in a blender; return to pan. Add evaporated milk and cheese; cook and stir for 3-5 minutes or until the cheese is melted. If desired, sprinkle each serving with additional cheese and thyme.

CHEDDAR, CORN & POTATO CHOWDER

Curry gives this soup the right amount of zip without being overpowering. I especially like all the veggies in the recipe! I always make a double or triple batch so we have plenty of leftovers.
—**BECKY RUFF** MCGREGOR, IA

PREP: 15 MIN. • **COOK:** 35 MIN. • **MAKES:** 6 SERVINGS

- ¼ **cup butter, cubed**
- 2 **celery ribs, chopped**
- 2 **medium carrots, sliced**
- 1 **medium green pepper, finely chopped**
- 1 **medium onion, chopped**
- ¼ **cup all-purpose flour**
- 1 **teaspoon curry powder**
- ½ **teaspoon salt**
- ¼ **teaspoon pepper**
- 1 **cup 2% milk**
- 1 **carton (32 ounces) chicken broth**
- 1 **pound potatoes (about 2 medium), peeled and cubed**
- 1 **can (8¾ ounces) whole kernel corn, drained**
- 2 **cups shredded cheddar cheese**
- 1 **tablespoon minced fresh parsley**

1. In a 6-qt. stockpot, heat butter over medium heat. Add celery, carrots, green pepper and onion; cook and stir for 3-4 minutes or until the onion is tender. Stir in flour and seasonings until blended.

2. Gradually stir in milk. Add broth, potatoes and corn; bring to a boil. Reduce heat; simmer, covered, for 15-20 minutes or until the potatoes are tender.

3. Stir in cheese until melted; remove from heat. Puree soup using an immersion blender. Or, cool the soup slightly and puree in batches in a blender; return to pot and heat through. Stir in parsley and serve, or sprinkle parsley over individual servings.

HOT DOG CHOWDER

We have 23 grandchildren and have found they love this recipe whenever I serve it. The change-of-pace meal features hearty hash browns and vegetables, too.
—CAROLYN ZIMMERMAN FAIRBURY, IL

PREP: 10 MIN. • **COOK:** 35 MIN.
MAKES: 8 SERVINGS (2 QUARTS)

- 2 **cups frozen cubed hash brown potatoes, thawed**
- 1 **package (10 ounces) frozen mixed vegetables, thawed and drained**
- 1 **cup water**
- ¼ **cup chopped onion**
- 3 **teaspoons chicken bouillon granules**
- 3 **teaspoons minced fresh parsley**
- ½ **teaspoon salt**
- ⅛ **teaspoon pepper**
- 6 **hot dogs, sliced**
- 3 **cups milk**
- ¼ **cup all-purpose flour**
- 2 **tablespoons butter**

1. In a large saucepan, combine the first eight ingredients. Bring to a boil. Reduce heat; cover and simmer for 15 minutes.

2. Stir in hot dog slices and 2½ cups of the milk. Combine flour and the remaining milk until smooth. Stir into soup. Bring to a boil; cook and stir for 2 minutes or until thickened. Stir in butter until melted.

FRESH ASPARAGUS SOUP

We have a large asparagus patch and are able to freeze a lot for the year. This recipe highlights all the flavor of the vegetable and is easy to make. I like to heat up some soup in a coffee mug for an afternoon snack.

—SHERRI MELOTIK OAK CREEK, WI

PREP: 15 MIN. • **COOK:** 20 MIN. • **MAKES:** 6 SERVINGS

- 1 **teaspoon canola oil**
- 1 **small onion, chopped**
- 1 **garlic clove, minced**
- 2 **pounds fresh asparagus, trimmed and cut into 1-inch pieces (about 5 cups)**
- 1 **can (14½ ounces) reduced-sodium chicken broth**
- 4 **tablespoons all-purpose flour, divided**
- 2½ **cups fat-free milk, divided**
- 2 **tablespoons butter**
- ¾ **teaspoon salt**
- ⅛ **teaspoon dried thyme**
- ⅛ **teaspoon pepper**
- ½ **cup half-and-half cream**
- 2 **tablespoons white wine**
- 1 **tablespoon lemon juice**
  Minced fresh chives, optional

1. In a large saucepan, heat oil over medium heat. Add onion; cook and stir for 4-6 minutes or until tender. Add garlic; cook 1 minute longer. Add asparagus and broth; bring to a boil. Reduce heat; simmer, uncovered, for 8-10 minutes or until the asparagus is tender. Remove from heat; cool slightly. Transfer to a blender; cover and process until smooth.

2. In a small bowl, mix 2 tablespoons of the flour and ¼ cup of the milk until smooth; set aside. In same saucepan, heat butter over medium heat. Stir in seasonings and the remaining flour until smooth; cook and stir 45-60 seconds or until light golden brown. Gradually whisk in cream, the remaining milk and reserved flour mixture. Bring to a boil, stirring constantly; cook and stir 1-2 minutes or until thickened. Stir in wine, lemon juice and asparagus mixture; heat through. If desired, top each serving with chives.

POTATO, SAUSAGE & KALE SOUP

I let my young son pick out seed packets and he chose kale, which grew like crazy. This soup helped make good use of it and rivals a restaurant version that we love.

—MICHELLE BABBIE MALONE, NY

START TO FINISH: 30 MIN. • **MAKES:** 4 SERVINGS

- ½ **pound bulk pork sausage**
- 1 **medium onion, finely chopped**
- 2 **teaspoons chicken bouillon granules**
- ½ **teaspoon garlic powder**
- ½ **teaspoon pepper**
- 2 **medium red potatoes, cut into ½-inch cubes**
- 2 **cups sliced fresh kale**
- 3 **cups 2% milk**
- 1 **cup heavy whipping cream**
- 1 **tablespoon cornstarch**
- ¼ **cup cold water**

1. In a large saucepan, cook sausage and onion over medium heat for 4-6 minutes or until the sausage is no longer pink and the onion is tender, breaking up sausage into crumbles; drain.

2. Stir in seasonings. Add potatoes, kale, milk and cream; bring to a boil. Reduce heat; simmer, covered, 10-15 minutes or until the potatoes are tender.

3. In a small bowl, mix cornstarch and water until smooth; stir into soup. Return to a boil, stirring constantly; cook and stir for 1-2 minutes or until thickened.

NOTES

VEGGIE CHOWDER

PREP: 10 MIN. • **COOK:** 35 MIN. • **MAKES:** 4 SERVINGS

- 4 **bacon strips, diced**
- ½ **cup chopped onion**
- 2 **medium red potatoes, cubed**
- 2 **small carrots, halved lengthwise and thinly sliced**
- 1 **cup water**
- 1½ **teaspoons chicken bouillon granules**
- 2 **cups whole milk**
- 1⅓ **cups frozen corn**
- ¼ **teaspoon pepper**
- 2 **tablespoons all-purpose flour**
- ¼ **cup cold water**
- 1¼ **cups shredded cheddar cheese**

1. In a large saucepan, cook bacon over medium heat until crisp. Remove to paper towels with a slotted spoon; drain, reserving 2 teaspoons drippings.

2. Saute onion in the drippings until tender. Add potatoes, carrots, water and bouillon. Bring to a boil. Reduce heat; cover and simmer for 15-20 minutes or until the vegetables are almost tender.

3. Stir in milk, corn and pepper. Cook for 5 minutes longer. Combine flour and cold water until smooth; gradually stir into soup. Bring to a boil; cook and stir for 1-2 minutes or until thickened. Remove from the heat; stir in cheese until melted. Sprinkle with bacon.

When the weather turns brisk, we enjoy
soothing foods like this chowder.
It's easy to prepare, and the aroma
will make your mouth water.

—**SHEENA HOFFMAN** NORTH VANCOUVER, BC

ROASTED TOMATO BISQUE

Just before the first frost of the season, we gather up all of the tomatoes from my mom's garden to create this flavorful soup. Although it sounds like a lot of garlic, when it's roasted, the garlic becomes mellow and almost sweet. We serve this soup with toasted bread spread with pesto.

—**KAITLYN LERDAHL** MADISON, WI

PREP: 25 MIN. • **COOK:** 40 MIN. • **MAKES:** 6 SERVINGS

15 **large tomatoes (5 pounds), seeded and quartered**
¼ **cup plus 2 tablespoons canola oil, divided**
8 **garlic cloves, minced**
1 **large onion, chopped**
2 **cups water**
1 **teaspoon salt**
½ **teaspoon crushed red pepper flakes, optional**
½ **cup heavy whipping cream**
   Fresh basil leaves, optional

1. Preheat oven to 400°. Place the tomatoes in a greased 15x10x1-in. baking pan. Combine ¼ cup oil and garlic; drizzle over the tomatoes. Toss to coat. Bake for 15-20 minutes or until softened, stirring occasionally. Remove and discard the skins.

2. Meanwhile, in a Dutch oven, saute onion in the remaining oil until tender. Add tomatoes and garlic, water, salt and, if desired, red pepper flakes. Bring to a boil. Reduce heat; cover and simmer for 30 minutes or until the flavors are blended. Cool slightly.

3. In a blender, process the soup in batches until smooth. Return to the pan. Stir in cream and heat through. Sprinkle with basil if desired.

FREEZER OPTION *Cool soup and transfer to freezer containers. Freeze up to 3 months. To use, thaw in the refrigerator overnight. Place in a large saucepan; heat through. Garnish with basil if desired.*

CRAB SOUP WITH SHERRY

PREP: 15 MIN. • **COOK:** 30 MIN.
MAKES: 6 SERVINGS

- 1 **pound fresh or frozen crabmeat, thawed**
- 6 **tablespoons sherry or chicken broth**
- 1 **small onion, grated**
- ¼ **cup butter, cubed**
- ¼ **cup all-purpose flour**
- ½ **teaspoon salt**
- 2 **cups 2% milk**
- 2 **chicken bouillon cubes**
- 3 **cups half-and-half cream**
- 2 **tablespoons minced fresh parsley**

1. In a small bowl, combine crabmeat and sherry; set aside.

2. In a large saucepan, saute onion in butter until tender. Stir in flour and salt until blended; gradually add milk and bouillon. Bring to a boil; cook and stir for 2 minutes or until thickened. Stir in the cream and crab mixture; heat through. Sprinkle individual servings with parsley.

> Everybody loves this rich, comforting soup that's a tradition in the South. It has a smooth texture and is brimming with crab.
>
> —REGINA HUGGINS SUMMERVILLE, SC

CREAMY CHICKEN GNOCCHI SOUP

Warm up on a snowy evening by enjoying a bowl of this chicken and pasta soup. It's quick to fix and loved by all who try it.

—JACLYNN ROBINSON SHINGLETOWN, CA

PREP: 25 MIN. • **COOK:** 15 MIN. • **MAKES:** 8 SERVINGS (2 QUARTS)

- 1 **pound boneless skinless chicken breasts, cut into ½-inch pieces**
- ⅓ **cup butter, divided**
- 1 **small onion, chopped**
- 1 **medium carrot, shredded**
- 1 **celery rib, chopped**
- 2 **garlic cloves, minced**
- ⅓ **cup all-purpose flour**
- 3½ **cups 2% milk**
- 1½ **cups heavy whipping cream**
- 1 **tablespoon reduced-sodium chicken bouillon granules**
- ¼ **teaspoon coarsely ground pepper**
- 1 **package (16 ounces) potato gnocchi**
- ½ **cup chopped fresh spinach**

1. In a Dutch oven, brown chicken in 2 tablespoons butter. Remove and keep warm. In the same pan, saute the onion, carrot, celery and garlic in remaining butter until tender.

2. Whisk in flour until blended; gradually stir in the milk, cream, bouillon and pepper. Bring to a boil. Reduce heat; cook and stir for 2 minutes or until thickened.

3. Add the gnocchi and spinach; cook for 3-4 minutes or until the spinach is wilted. Add the chicken. Cover and simmer for 10 minutes or until heated through (do not boil).

NOTE *Look for potato gnocchi in the pasta or frozen foods section of the grocery store.*

SOUTHWESTERN BEAN CHOWDER

Even though there is a bit of heat from the spices and green chilies, my young children love this soup as much as my husband does. I like using white kidney beans—they have a terrific texture.
—**JULI MEYERS** HINESVILLE, GA

PREP: 20 MIN. • **COOK:** 35 MIN.
MAKES: 8 SERVINGS (2 QUARTS)

- **2 cans (15 ounces each) white kidney or cannellini beans, rinsed and drained, divided**
- **1 medium onion, chopped**
- **¼ cup chopped celery**
- **¼ cup chopped green pepper**
- **1 tablespoon olive oil**
- **2 garlic cloves, minced**
- **3 cups vegetable broth**
- **1½ cups frozen corn, thawed**
- **1 medium carrot, shredded**
- **1 can (4 ounces) chopped green chilies**
- **1 tablespoon ground cumin**
- **½ teaspoon chili powder**
- **4½ teaspoons cornstarch**
- **2 cups 2% milk**
- **1 cup shredded cheddar cheese**
  Minced fresh cilantro and additional shredded cheddar cheese, optional

1. In a small bowl, mash one can of beans with a fork; set aside.
2. In a Dutch oven, saute the onion, celery and pepper in oil until tender. Add garlic; cook 1 minute longer. Stir in the mashed beans, broth, corn, carrot, chilies, cumin, chili powder and remaining beans. Bring to a boil. Reduce heat; simmer, uncovered, for 20 minutes.
3. Combine cornstarch and milk until smooth. Stir into bean mixture. Bring to a boil; cook and stir for 2 minutes or until thickened. Stir in cheese until melted. Serve with cilantro and additional cheese if desired.

CREAMY BUTTERNUT SQUASH & SAGE SOUP

I recently started experimenting with new soup recipes, and finally created a rich squash version that omits heavy cream altogether, making it a healthier way to curb my creamy-tooth.
—**NITHYA KUMAR** DAVIS, CA

PREP: 20 MIN. • **COOK:** 50 MIN. • **MAKES:** 4 SERVINGS

- 4 **cups cubed peeled butternut squash**
- 1 **tablespoon olive oil**
- 2 **tablespoons minced fresh sage**
- ¼ **teaspoon salt**
- ¼ **teaspoon pepper**

SOUP

- 1 **tablespoon olive oil**
- 2 **tablespoons butter, divided**
- 1 **medium onion, chopped**
- 1 **garlic clove, minced**
- ¾ **teaspoon salt**
- ¼ **to ½ teaspoon crushed red pepper flakes**
- ⅛ **teaspoon pepper**
- 4 **cups water**
- 1 **medium sweet potato, chopped**
- 1 **medium carrot, chopped**

1. Preheat oven to 400°. Place the squash in a foil-lined 15x10x1-in. baking pan. Drizzle with oil; sprinkle with sage, salt and pepper. Toss to coat. Roast for 30-35 minutes or until tender, stirring occasionally.

2. Meanwhile, in a large saucepan, heat oil and 1 tablespoon butter over medium heat. Add onion and garlic; cook and stir for 3-4 minutes or until softened. Reduce heat to medium-low; cook for 30-40 minutes or until deep golden brown, stirring occasionally. Stir in salt, pepper flakes and pepper.

3. Add water, sweet potato and carrot to saucepan. Bring to a boil. Reduce heat; cook, uncovered, for 10-15 minutes or until the vegetables are tender. Add the squash mixture and remaining butter to soup. Puree soup using an immersion blender. Or, cool soup slightly and puree in batches in a blender; return to pan and heat through.

FRESH CORN & POTATO CHOWDER

PREP: 15 MIN. • **COOK:** 25 MIN. • **MAKES:** 6 SERVINGS

- 1 **tablespoon butter**
- 1 **medium onion, chopped**
- 1 **pound red potatoes (about 3 medium), cubed**
- 1½ **cups fresh or frozen corn (about 7 ounces)**
- 3 **cups reduced-sodium chicken broth**
- 1¼ **cups half-and-half cream, divided**
- 2 **green onions, thinly sliced**
- ½ **teaspoon salt**
- ¼ **teaspoon freshly ground pepper**
- 3 **tablespoons all-purpose flour**
- 1 **tablespoon minced fresh parsley**

1. In a large saucepan, heat butter over medium-high heat. Add onion; cook and stir for 2-4 minutes or until tender. Add potatoes, corn, broth, 1 cup cream, green onions, salt and pepper; bring to a boil. Reduce heat; simmer, covered, for 12-15 minutes or until the potatoes are tender.

2. In a small bowl, mix flour and remaining cream until smooth; stir into soup. Return to a boil, stirring constantly; cook and stir for 1-2 minutes or until slightly thickened. Stir in parsley.

This soup was one of my favorites as a child in upstate New York, and I still love it to this day. For extra depth, place the spent corn cob in the soup, simmer, then remove.

—TRACY BIVINS KNOB NOSTER, MO

HELPFUL HINT

The skin of celery root is too thick for a vegetable peeler; use a knife. Place the celery root on its side and cut off the top and bottom. Then set the root on one of its now-flat sides and cut off the skin in vertical strips.

CREAMY ROOT VEGGIE SOUP

For chilly nights, we fill the pot with parsnips and celery root for a smooth, creamy soup flavored with garlic, bacon and thyme.
—**SALLY SIBTHORPE** SHELBY TOWNSHIP, MI

PREP: 15 MIN. • **COOK:** 1 HOUR • **MAKES:** 8 SERVINGS

- 4 **bacon strips, chopped**
- 1 **large onion, chopped**
- 3 **garlic cloves, minced**
- 1 **large celery root, peeled and cubed (about 5 cups)**
- 6 **medium parsnips, peeled and cubed (about 4 cups)**
- 6 **cups chicken stock**
- 1 **bay leaf**
- 1 **cup heavy whipping cream**
- 2 **teaspoons minced fresh thyme**
- 1 **teaspoon salt**
- ¼ **teaspoon white pepper**
- ¼ **teaspoon ground nutmeg**
  Additional minced fresh thyme

1. In a Dutch oven, cook bacon over medium heat until crisp, stirring occasionally. Remove with a slotted spoon; drain on paper towels. Cook and stir onion in bacon drippings for 6-8 minutes or until tender. Add garlic; cook 1 minute longer.

2. Add celery root, parsnips, stock and bay leaf. Bring to a boil. Reduce heat; cook, uncovered, 30-40 minutes or until the vegetables are tender. Remove the bay leaf.

3. Puree soup using an immersion blender. Or, cool slightly and puree in batches in a blender; return to pan. Stir in cream, 2 teaspoons thyme, salt, pepper and nutmeg; heat through. Top each serving with bacon and additional thyme.

SWEET POTATO BISQUE

I love to serve my bright orange bisque on special occasions. Making the minted chili oil to drizzle on top takes a few extra minutes but is well worth it.

—LILY JULOW LAWRENCEVILLE, GA

PREP: 30 MIN. • **COOK:** 40 MIN.
MAKES: 8 SERVINGS (2 QUARTS)

- **8 bacon strips, finely chopped**
- **6 medium carrots, chopped (2 cups)**
- **1 medium onion, chopped (1 cup)**
- **3 garlic cloves, minced**
- **3 cups water**
- **1¾ pounds sweet potatoes (about 4 medium), peeled and cubed**
- **3 bay leaves**
- **2½ teaspoons curry powder**
- **¾ teaspoon salt**
- **½ teaspoon ground cinnamon**
- **½ teaspoon smoked paprika**
- **½ teaspoon pepper**
- **1½ cups heavy whipping cream**
- **1 cup (8 ounces) sour cream**

MINTED CHILI OIL

- **18 mint sprigs, chopped**
- **3 tablespoons olive oil**
- **¼ teaspoon sugar**
- **¼ teaspoon salt**
- **¼ teaspoon crushed red pepper flakes**
- **¼ teaspoon pepper**

1. In a large saucepan, cook bacon over medium heat until crisp, stirring occasionally. Remove with a slotted spoon; drain on paper towels. Discard drippings, reserving 2 tablespoons in the pan.

2. Add carrots and onion to the drippings; cook and stir over medium-high heat until the vegetables are tender. Add garlic; cook 1 minute longer.

3. Stir in water, sweet potatoes, bay leaves, curry, salt, cinnamon, paprika and pepper. Bring to a boil. Reduce heat; simmer, covered, 10-15 minutes or until the vegetables are tender. Discard bay leaves. Stir in cream and sour cream just until blended. Cool.

4. Meanwhile, in a small bowl, combine mint, oil, sugar, salt, red pepper flakes and pepper. Let stand for 5-10 minutes.

5. Process bisque in batches in a blender until smooth; return all to the pan. Heat through (do not boil). Ladle the bisque into bowls; drizzle each serving with minted chili oil.

ANDOUILLE-SHRIMP CREAM SOUP

Inspired by southern Louisiana corn stew, this soup contains a wonderful blend of andouille sausage, shrimp and subtle spices.
—**JUDY ARMSTRONG** PRAIRIEVILLE, LA

PREP: 20 MIN. • **COOK:** 30 MIN. • **MAKES:** 7 SERVINGS

- ½ **pound fully cooked andouille sausage links, thinly sliced**
- 1 **medium onion, chopped**
- 2 **celery ribs, thinly sliced**
- 1 **medium sweet red pepper, chopped**
- 1 **medium green pepper, chopped**
- 1 **jalapeno pepper, seeded and chopped**
- ¼ **cup butter, cubed**
- 3 **garlic cloves, minced**
- 2 **cups fresh or frozen corn, thawed**
- 4 **plum tomatoes, chopped**
- 1 **cup vegetable broth**
- 2 **tablespoons minced fresh thyme or 2 teaspoons dried thyme**
- 1 **teaspoon chili powder**
- ½ **teaspoon salt**
- ½ **teaspoon pepper**
- ¼ **to ½ teaspoon cayenne pepper**
- 1 **pound uncooked medium shrimp, peeled and deveined**
- 1 **cup heavy whipping cream**

1. In a large skillet, saute the first six ingredients in butter until the vegetables are tender. Add garlic; cook 1 minute longer. Add corn, tomatoes, broth, thyme, chili powder, salt, pepper and cayenne. Bring to a boil. Reduce heat; simmer, uncovered, for 10 minutes.

2. Stir in shrimp and cream. Bring to a gentle boil. Simmer, uncovered, for 8-10 minutes or until the shrimp turn pink.

NOTE *Wear disposable gloves when cutting hot peppers; the oils can burn skin. Avoid touching your face.*

GARLICKY CHEDDAR CHEESE BISQUE

I give classic cheddar cheese soup a boost with a variety of root vegetables. Crushed pita chips and fresh parsley make fun garnishes.
—PATRICIA HARMON BADEN, PA

PREP: 30 MIN. • **COOK:** 40 MIN. • **MAKES:** 6 SERVINGS

- 1 **tablespoon butter**
- 1 **tablespoon canola oil**
- 1 **medium leek (white portion only), sliced**
- ½ **cup chopped carrot**
- ½ **cup chopped celery**
- ½ **cup chopped peeled parsnip**
- 1 **teaspoon salt**
- ½ **teaspoon pepper**
- 6 **garlic cloves, minced**
- 2 **cans (14½ ounces each) chicken broth**
- ⅔ **cup dry white wine**
- 2 **tablespoons cornstarch**
- ¼ **cup cold water**
- 1 **can (12 ounces) evaporated milk**
- 2 **cups shredded sharp white cheddar cheese**
  Crushed baked pita chips
  Minced fresh parsley

1. In a large saucepan, heat butter and oil over medium heat. Add vegetables, salt and pepper; cook and stir for 7-8 minutes or until the vegetables are crisp-tender. Add garlic; cook for 1-2 minutes longer.

2. Stir in broth and wine; bring to a boil. Reduce heat; simmer, uncovered, for 15-20 minutes or until the vegetables are tender. Remove from heat; cool slightly. Meanwhile, in a small bowl, mix cornstarch and water until smooth.

3. Process soup in batches in a food processor until smooth. Return all to pan. Stir in evaporated milk and cornstarch mixture; bring to a boil. Reduce heat; simmer, uncovered, until thickened and bubbly, stirring frequently. Add cheese; cook and stir until cheese is blended. Top each serving with crushed pita chips and parsley.

HOMEMADE CREAM OF MUSHROOM SOUP

Blow away friends and family with this rich blend of shiitake and portobello mushrooms. You will never want to eat canned soup again.

—MICHAEL WILLIAMS
MORENO VALLEY, CA

PREP: 40 MIN. • **COOK:** 50 MIN.
MAKES: 8 SERVINGS (2 QUARTS)

- ½ **pound fresh shiitake mushrooms**
- ½ **pound baby portobello mushrooms**
- 1 **medium onion, chopped**
- 1 **medium carrot, chopped**
- 1 **tablespoon olive oil**
- 1 **tablespoon plus ½ cup butter, divided**
- 5 **cups water**
- 1 **fresh thyme sprig**
- 1¼ **teaspoons salt, divided**
- ¾ **teaspoon coarsely ground pepper, divided**
- 2 **cups chopped leeks (white portion only)**
- ¼ **cup all-purpose flour**
- 1 **cup white wine or chicken broth**
- 1 **teaspoon minced fresh thyme**
- 1 **cup heavy whipping cream**
- 1 **cup half-and-half cream**
- ½ **cup minced fresh parsley**

1. Remove the mushroom stems and coarsely chop them. Slice the mushroom caps into ¼-in. slices and set aside.

2. In a large saucepan, cook onion, carrot and the mushroom stems in oil and 1 tablespoon butter over medium heat until the vegetables are tender. Stir in the water, thyme sprig, ½ teaspoon salt and ¼ teaspoon pepper. Bring to a boil. Reduce heat; simmer, uncovered, for 30 minutes. Strain the broth, discarding the vegetables and seasonings. Set aside 4½ cups broth.

3. In a Dutch oven, cook leeks in the remaining butter over low heat for 25-30 minutes or just until the leeks begin to brown, stirring occasionally. Stir in the mushroom caps; cook 10 minutes longer or until the mushrooms are tender.

4. Stir in flour until blended; gradually add wine. Stir in the thyme, remaining salt and pepper and reserved broth. Bring to a boil; cook and stir for 2 minutes or until thickened. Stir in the creams and parsley; heat through (do not boil).

PUMPKIN BISQUE WITH SMOKED GOUDA

PREP: 20 MIN. • **COOK:** 35 MIN.
MAKES: 9 SERVINGS (2¼ QUARTS)

- 4 **bacon strips, chopped**
- 1 **medium onion, chopped**
- 3 **garlic cloves, minced**
- 6 **cups chicken broth**
- 1 **can (29 ounces) solid-pack pumpkin**
- ½ **teaspoon salt**
- ¼ **teaspoon ground nutmeg**
- ⅛ **teaspoon pepper**
- 1 **cup heavy whipping cream**
- 1 **cup shredded Gouda cheese**
- 2 **tablespoons minced fresh parsley**
  Additional shredded Gouda cheese, optional

1. In a Dutch oven, cook bacon over medium heat until crisp. Remove to paper towels with a slotted spoon; drain, reserving 1 tablespoon drippings. Saute onion in the reserved drippings until tender. Add garlic; cook 1 minute longer.

2. Stir in the broth, pumpkin, salt, nutmeg and pepper. Bring to a boil. Reduce heat; simmer, uncovered, for 10 minutes. Cool slightly.

3. In a blender, process soup in batches until smooth. Return all to pan. Stir in cream; heat through. Add cheese; stir until melted. Sprinkle each serving with parsley, bacon and, if desired, additional cheese.

I love the smell of this rich, cheesy soup as it bubbles on the stove. The Gouda adds a delightful smokiness that just says autumn to me.

—KERRY DINGWALL PONTE VEDRA, FL

TURKEY & WILD RICE SOUP

A dear friend shared this recipe with me several years ago before she passed and I've been making it my own ever since. I make this soup whenever I think of her. Sometimes I will add a cup of cheddar cheese at the end and melt it in for an extra measure of comfort.
—**CAROL BRAULT** HENDERSON, NC

PREP: 20 MIN. • **COOK:** 65 MIN.
MAKES: 8 SERVINGS (2½ QUARTS)

- ½ **cup uncooked wild rice**
- 4 **cups water**
- ½ **cup butter, cubed**
- 8 **ounces red potatoes (about 2 medium), chopped**
- 1 **medium onion, chopped**
- 1 **celery rib, chopped**
- 1 **medium carrot, chopped**
- 2 **garlic cloves, minced**
- ½ **cup all-purpose flour**
- 3 **cups chicken broth**
- 2 **cups half-and-half cream**
- 1 **teaspoon salt**
- ½ **teaspoon dried rosemary, crushed**
- 2 **cups cubed cooked turkey or chicken**

1. In a saucepan, combine rice and water; bring to a boil over high heat. Reduce heat; simmer, covered, 30 minutes.

2. Meanwhile, in a Dutch oven, heat butter over medium heat. Add potatoes, onion, celery and carrot; cook and stir for 6-8 minutes or until almost tender. Add garlic; cook 1 minute longer.

3. Stir in flour until blended; cook and stir for 2 minutes. Gradually stir in the broth and undrained rice. Bring to a boil over medium-high heat; cook and stir for 1-2 minutes or until slightly thickened.

4. Add cream, salt and rosemary; return to a boil. Simmer, uncovered, for 15-20 minutes or until the rice is tender, stirring occasionally. Stir in turkey; heat through.

STEWS &
CHILI

BEEFY CABBAGE BEAN STEW

While we were on one of our small group quilting retreats, one of my friends made this wonderful recipe for dinner. We all loved it and have since passed it around for others to enjoy—now I'm passing it on to you.
—**MELISSA GLANCY** LA GRANGE, KY

PREP: 20 MIN. • **COOK:** 6 HOURS
MAKES: 6 SERVINGS

- ½ **pound lean ground beef (90% lean)**
- 3 **cups shredded cabbage or angel hair coleslaw mix**
- 1 **can (16 ounces) red beans, rinsed and drained**
- 1 **can (14½ ounces) diced tomatoes, undrained**
- 1 **can (8 ounces) tomato sauce**
- ¾ **cup salsa or picante sauce**
- 1 **medium green pepper, chopped**
- 1 **small onion, chopped**
- 3 **garlic cloves, minced**
- 1 **teaspoon ground cumin**
- ½ **teaspoon pepper**

1. In a large skillet, cook beef over medium heat for 4-6 minutes or until no longer pink, breaking into crumbles; drain.

2. Transfer the beef to a 4-qt. slow cooker. Stir in remaining ingredients. Cook, covered, on low for 6-8 hours or until the cabbage is tender.

TUSCAN PORTOBELLO STEW

This is a one-skillet meal that is quick and easy to prepare yet elegant enough for company. I take this to my school's potlucks, where it is devoured by teachers and students alike.
—**JANE SIEMON** VIROQUA, WI

PREP: 20 MIN. • **COOK:** 20 MIN. • **MAKES:** 4 SERVINGS

- 2 **large portobello mushrooms, coarsely chopped**
- 1 **medium onion, chopped**
- 3 **garlic cloves, minced**
- 2 **tablespoons olive oil**
- ½ **cup white wine or vegetable broth**
- 1 **can (28 ounces) diced tomatoes, undrained**
- 2 **cups chopped fresh kale**
- 1 **bay leaf**
- 1 **teaspoon dried thyme**
- ½ **teaspoon dried basil**
- ½ **teaspoon dried rosemary, crushed**
- ¼ **teaspoon salt**
- ¼ **teaspoon pepper**
- 2 **cans (15 ounces each) white kidney or cannellini beans, rinsed and drained**

1. In a large skillet, saute mushrooms, onion and garlic in oil until tender. Add the wine. Bring to a boil; cook until liquid is reduced by half. Stir in tomatoes, kale and seasonings. Bring to a boil. Reduce heat; cover and simmer for 8-10 minutes.
2. Add beans; heat through. Discard the bay leaf.

MARTY'S BEAN BURGER CHILI

PREP: 15 MIN. • **COOK:** 7 HOURS • **MAKES:** 6 SERVINGS

- 2 cans (14½ ounces each) no-salt-added diced tomatoes, drained
- 1 can (14½ ounces) diced tomatoes, drained
- 1 can (16 ounces) kidney beans, undrained
- 1 can (15 ounces) black beans, undrained
- 1 can (15 ounces) garbanzo beans or chickpeas, rinsed and drained
- 4 frozen spicy black bean veggie burgers, thawed and coarsely chopped
- 1 large onion, finely chopped
- 1 large sweet red or green pepper, chopped
- 2 tablespoons chili powder
- 1 tablespoon Worcestershire sauce
- 3 teaspoons dried basil
- 3 teaspoons dried oregano
- 2 teaspoons hot pepper sauce
- 2 garlic cloves, minced

Place all ingredients in a 5- or 6-qt. slow cooker; stir to combine. Cook, covered, on low for 7-9 hours to allow the flavors to blend.

My husband and I met while working the dinner shift at a homeless shelter where they served my chili. I've revised the chili using veggie bean burgers.

—**MRS. MARTY NICKERSON** ELLINGTON, CT

MOROCCAN VEGETARIAN STEW

This fragrant, spicy stew can also be served over couscous or with a warm pita bread. Try topping it with a dollop of plain yogurt or sour cream to cool it down.
—SONYA LABBE WEST HOLLYWOOD, CA

PREP: 20 MIN. • **COOK:** 30 MIN. • **MAKES:** 8 SERVINGS (3 QUARTS)

- 1 **large onion, chopped**
- 1 **tablespoon olive oil**
- 2 **teaspoons ground cinnamon**
- 2 **teaspoons ground cumin**
- 1 **teaspoon ground coriander**
- ½ **teaspoon cayenne pepper**
- ½ **teaspoon ground allspice**
- ¼ **teaspoon salt**
- 3 **cups water**
- 1 **small butternut squash, peeled and cubed**
- 2 **medium potatoes, peeled and cubed**
- 4 **medium carrots, sliced**
- 3 **plum tomatoes, chopped**
- 2 **small zucchini, cut into 1-inch pieces**
- 1 **can (15 ounces) garbanzo beans or chickpeas, rinsed and drained**

1. In a Dutch oven, saute onion in oil until tender. Add spices and salt; cook 1 minute longer.

2. Stir in water, squash, potatoes, carrots and tomatoes. Bring to a boil. Reduce heat; simmer, uncovered, for 15-20 minutes or until the potatoes and squash are almost tender.

3. Add zucchini and garbanzo beans; return to a boil. Reduce heat; simmer, uncovered, for 5-8 minutes or until the vegetables are tender.

FREEZE OPTION *Prepare soup as directed, reserving potatoes for later. Freeze cooled soup in freezer containers. To use, partially thaw in refrigerator overnight. Transfer soup to a Dutch oven. Add potatoes; simmer until potatoes are tender, stirring occasionally and adding a little water if necessary.*

HELPFUL HINT

Coriander and cumin are sold in both ground and seed form. If time allows, grind the seeds yourself to give the spice a fresher flavor. As an extra step, toasting the seeds before grinding gives the spice a warm, roasted depth.

SLOW COOKER TURKEY CHILI

This chili is a quick meal to prepare in the morning and a delicious, wholesome dinner to return to in the evening.
—TERRI CRANDALL GARDNERVILLE, NV

PREP: 30 MIN. • **COOK:** 7¼ HOURS
MAKES: 8 SERVINGS (2¾ QUARTS)

- 2 **tablespoons olive oil**
- 1½ **pounds ground turkey**
- 1 **medium onion, chopped**
- 2 **tablespoons ground ancho chili pepper**
- 1 **tablespoon chili powder**
- 1½ **teaspoons salt**
- 1½ **teaspoons ground cumin**
- 1½ **teaspoons paprika**
- 2 **cans (14½ ounces each) fire-roasted diced tomatoes, undrained**
- 1 **medium sweet yellow pepper, chopped**
- 1 **medium sweet red pepper, chopped**
- 1 **can (4 ounces) chopped green chilies**
- 1 **garlic clove, minced**
- 1 **cup brewed coffee**
- ¾ **cup dry red wine or chicken broth**
- 1 **can (16 ounces) kidney beans, rinsed and drained**
- 1 **can (15 ounces) white kidney or cannellini beans, rinsed and drained**
   Sliced avocado and chopped green onions

1. In a large skillet, heat oil over medium heat. Add turkey and onion; cook for 8-10 minutes or until the meat is no longer pink, breaking up turkey into crumbles.

2. Transfer to a 5-qt. slow cooker; stir in seasonings. Add tomatoes, sweet peppers, chilies and garlic; stir in coffee and wine.

3. Cook, covered, on low for 7-9 hours. Stir in beans; cook 15-20 minutes longer or until heated through. Top each serving with avocado and green onions.

FREEZE OPTION *Cool and freeze in freezer containers. To use, partially thaw in refrigerator overnight. Heat in a saucepan, stirring occasionally, adding broth or water if necessary.*

PORK AND GREEN CHILE STEW

As an easily adaptable stew, this dish is ready in four hours if cooked on high in a slow cooker, or in eight hours if cooked low and slow.
—PAUL SEDILLO PLAINFIELD, IL

PREP: 40 MIN. • **COOK:** 7 HOURS
MAKES: 8 SERVINGS (2 QUARTS)

- 2 pounds boneless pork shoulder butt roast, cut into ¾-inch cubes
- 1 large onion, cut into ½-in. pieces
- 2 tablespoons canola oil
- 1 teaspoon salt
- 1 teaspoon coarsely ground pepper
- 4 large potatoes, peeled and cut into ¾-inch cubes
- 3 cups water
- 1 can (16 ounces) hominy, rinsed and drained
- 2 cans (4 ounces each) chopped green chilies
- 2 tablespoons quick-cooking tapioca
- 2 garlic cloves, minced
- ½ teaspoon dried oregano
- ½ teaspoon ground cumin
- 1 cup minced fresh cilantro
  Sour cream, optional

1. In a large skillet, brown pork and onion in oil in batches. Sprinkle with salt and pepper. Transfer to a 4-qt. slow cooker.
2. Stir in potatoes, water, hominy, chilies, tapioca, garlic, oregano and cumin. Cover and cook on low for 7-9 hours or until the meat is tender, stirring in cilantro during the last 30 minutes of cooking. Serve with sour cream if desired.

BEER BRAT CHILI

My husband and I love this chili because it smells so good as it simmers in the slow cooker all day. I can't think of a better way to use up leftover brats; he can't think of a better way to eat them!

—KATRINA KRUMM APPLE VALLEY, MN

PREP: 10 MIN. • **COOK:** 5 HOURS
MAKES: 8 SERVINGS (2 ½ QUARTS)

- **1 can (15 ounces) white kidney or cannellini beans, rinsed and drained**
- **1 can (15 ounces) pinto beans, rinsed and drained**
- **1 can (15 ounces) Southwestern black beans, undrained**
- **1 can (14½ ounces) Italian diced tomatoes, undrained**
- **1 can (10 ounces) diced tomatoes and green chilies, undrained**
- **1 package (14 ounces) fully cooked beer bratwurst links, sliced**
- **1½ cups frozen corn**
- **1 medium sweet red pepper, chopped**
- **1 medium onion, finely chopped**
- **¼ cup chili seasoning mix**
- **1 garlic clove, minced**

In a 5-qt. slow cooker, combine all ingredients. Cook, covered, on low for 5-6 hours.

WHITE CHILI

My friend and I came up with this delicious slow-cooked chicken chili. The Alfredo sauce base makes it stand apart from other white chilis. Reduce the amount of cayenne pepper if you'd like a little less heat.

—CINDI MITCHELL ST. MARYS, KS

PREP: 30 MIN. • **COOK:** 3 HOURS
MAKES: 12 SERVINGS (1 CUP EACH)

- 3 cans (15½ ounces each) great northern beans, rinsed and drained
- 3 cups cubed cooked chicken breast
- 1 jar (15 ounces) Alfredo sauce
- 2 cups chicken broth
- 1 to 2 cans (4 ounces each) chopped green chilies
- 1½ cups frozen gold and white corn
- 1 cup shredded Monterey Jack cheese
- 1 cup shredded pepper jack cheese
- 1 cup sour cream
- 1 small sweet yellow pepper, chopped
- 1 small onion, chopped
- 3 garlic cloves, minced
- 1 tablespoon ground cumin
- 1½ teaspoons white pepper
- 1 to 1½ teaspoons cayenne pepper
  Salsa verde and chopped fresh cilantro, optional

In a 5- or 6-qt. slow cooker, combine the first 15 ingredients. Cover and cook on low for 3-4 hours or until heated though, stirring once. Serve with salsa verde and cilantro if desired.

TACO STEW

START TO FINISH: 30 MIN. • **MAKES:** 6 SERVINGS

- **1 pound ground beef**
- **2 cans (15 ounces each) black beans, rinsed and drained**
- **2 cans (10 ounces each) diced tomatoes and green chilies**
- **1 can (15 ounces) tomato sauce**
- **1½ cups frozen corn (about 7 ounces)**
- **2 teaspoons chili powder**
- **½ teaspoon ground cumin**
- **Crushed tortilla chips, optional**

1. In a large saucepan, cook beef over medium heat for 6-8 minutes or until no longer pink, breaking into crumbles; drain.

2. Stir in beans, tomatoes, tomato sauce, corn, chili powder and cumin. Bring to a boil. Reduce heat; simmer 5-10 minutes to allow flavors to blend. If desired, top each serving with tortilla chips.

FREEZE OPTION *Freeze cooled stew in freezer containers. To use, partially thaw in refrigerator overnight. Heat through in a saucepan, stirring occasionally and adding a little water if necessary.*

> The ingredients may be simple, but together they make an awesome stew. Crush a few tortilla chips on top of each bowl for added crunch.
>
> **—SUZANNE FRANCIS** MARYSVILLE, WA

QUINOA TURKEY CHILI

This heart-healthy chili is not only tasty, but it's a vitamin and protein powerhouse! Quinoa and beans are a nutritious way to stretch a half pound of turkey.

—SHARON GILJUM ARLINGTON, VA

PREP: 40 MIN. • **COOK:** 35 MIN.
MAKES: 9 SERVINGS (2¼ QUARTS)

- 1 **cup quinoa, rinsed**
- 3½ **cups water, divided**
- ½ **pound lean ground turkey**
- 1 **large sweet onion, chopped**
- 1 **medium sweet red pepper, chopped**
- 4 **garlic cloves, minced**
- 1 **tablespoon chili powder**
- 1 **tablespoon ground cumin**
- ½ **teaspoon ground cinnamon**
- 2 **cans (15 ounces each) black beans, rinsed and drained**
- 1 **can (28 ounces) crushed tomatoes**
- 1 **medium zucchini, chopped**
- 1 **chipotle pepper in adobo sauce, chopped**
- 1 **tablespoon adobo sauce**
- 1 **bay leaf**
- 1 **teaspoon dried oregano**
- ½ **teaspoon salt**
- ¼ **teaspoon pepper**
- 1 **cup frozen corn, thawed**
- ¼ **cup minced fresh cilantro**

1. In a large saucepan, bring the quinoa and 2 cups of water to a boil. Reduce the heat; cover and simmer for 12-15 minutes or until the water is absorbed. Remove from the heat; fluff with a fork and set aside.

2. Meanwhile, in a large saucepan coated with cooking spray, cook turkey, onion, red pepper and garlic over medium heat until the meat is no longer pink and the vegetables are tender; drain. Stir in chili powder, cumin and cinnamon; cook 2 minutes longer.

3. Add black beans, tomatoes, zucchini, chipotle pepper, adobo sauce, bay leaf, oregano, salt, pepper and the remaining water. Bring to a boil. Reduce heat; cover and simmer for 30 minutes. Stir in corn and quinoa; heat through. Discard the bay leaf; stir in cilantro.

FREEZE OPTION *Freeze cooled chili in freezer containers. To use, partially thaw in refrigerator overnight. Heat through in a saucepan, stirring occasionally and adding a little broth or water if necessary.*

NOTE *Look for quinoa in the cereal, rice or organic food aisle.*

OKRA AND BUTTER BEAN STEW

This stew is adapted from my mom's down-home Louisiana recipe. It turns okra haters into okra lovers—guaranteed!
—**KAYA MACK** WICHITA FALLS, TX

PREP: 25 MIN. • **COOK:** 45 MIN.
MAKES: 12 SERVINGS (1 CUP EACH)

- 7 bacon strips, chopped
- 1 pound smoked sausage, halved and thinly sliced
- 1 large onion, chopped
- 2 small green peppers, chopped
- 3 cups water
- 2 cans (16 ounces each) butter beans, rinsed and drained
- 1 can (14½ ounces) diced tomatoes, undrained
- 1 can (12 ounces) tomato paste
- 1 teaspoon pepper
- ¼ teaspoon salt
- 1 package (16 ounces) frozen sliced okra
  Hot cooked rice, optional

1. In a Dutch oven, cook bacon and sausage over medium heat until the bacon is crisp. Remove to paper towels; drain, reserving 2 tablespoons drippings.

2. Cook onion and green peppers in the drippings until tender. Stir in water, beans, tomatoes, tomato paste, pepper and salt. Bring to a boil. Reduce heat; simmer, uncovered, for 10 minutes. Add the bacon and sausage; cook for 10 minutes longer.

3. Stir in okra. Cover and cook for 8-10 minutes or until the okra is tender. Serve with rice if desired.

SWEET POTATO & BLACK BEAN CHILI

My whole family enjoys this vegetarian chili, but my daughter especially loves it. I like to make it because it's so easy and filled with flavor.

—JOY PENDLEY ORTONVILLE, MI

PREP: 25 MIN. • **COOK:** 35 MIN. • **MAKES:** 8 SERVINGS (2 QUARTS)

- 3 **large sweet potatoes, peeled and cut into ½-inch cubes**
- 1 **large onion, chopped**
- 1 **tablespoon olive oil**
- 2 **tablespoons chili powder**
- 3 **garlic cloves, minced**
- 1 **teaspoon ground cumin**
- ¼ **teaspoon cayenne pepper**
- 2 **cans (15 ounces each) black beans, rinsed and drained**
- 1 **can (28 ounces) diced tomatoes, undrained**
- ¼ **cup brewed coffee**
- 2 **tablespoons honey**
- ½ **teaspoon salt**
- ¼ **teaspoon pepper**
- ½ **cup shredded reduced-fat Monterey Jack cheese or reduced-fat Mexican cheese blend**

1. In a nonstick Dutch oven coated with cooking spray, saute sweet potatoes and onion in oil until crisp-tender. Add chili powder, garlic, cumin and cayenne; cook for 1 minute longer. Stir in beans, tomatoes, coffee, honey, salt and pepper.

2. Bring to a boil. Reduce heat; cover and simmer for 30-35 minutes or until the sweet potatoes are tender. Sprinkle each serving with cheese.

HELPFUL HINT

Outside of specialty shops, most of the "yams" sold in U.S. stores are really sweet potatoes. There are two common varieties of sweet potatoes: one has light yellow flesh; the other has dark orange flesh. The two are interchangeable in most recipes.

COMFORTING BEEF STEW

The aroma of slow-simmered stew that's loaded with root vegetables just says fall comfort food to me. Even my toddlers love to gobble up this stew!

—**COURTNEY PERCY** BROOKSVILLE, FL

PREP: 20 MIN. • **COOK:** 2½ HOURS • **MAKES:** 6 SERVINGS

- 2 **pounds beef stew meat**
- 1 **teaspoon salt**
- ¾ **teaspoon pepper**
- 3 **tablespoons canola oil**
- 1 **tablespoon butter**
- 1 **medium onion, chopped**
- 2 **garlic cloves, minced**
- ¼ **cup tomato paste**
- 4 **cups beef broth**
- 3 **tablespoons all-purpose flour**
- 3 **tablespoons water**
- 5 **medium carrots, cut into ½-inch pieces**
- 3 **medium turnips, peeled and cubed**
- 2 **tablespoons minced fresh parsley**

1. Sprinkle beef with salt and pepper. In a Dutch oven, heat oil over medium-high heat. Brown the beef in batches. Remove with a slotted spoon and set aside.

2. In same pot, heat butter over medium heat. Add onion; cook and stir for 2-3 minutes or until tender. Add garlic; cook 1 minute longer. Stir in tomato paste. Gradually stir in broth until blended. Return the beef to the pot; bring to a boil. Reduce heat; simmer, covered, for 1½ hours.

3. In a small bowl, mix flour and water until smooth; gradually stir into the stew. Add carrots and turnips; cook, covered, 30-40 minutes longer or until stew is thickened and the beef and vegetables are tender. Stir in parsley.

FREEZE OPTION *Freeze cooled stew in freezer containers. To use, partially thaw in refrigerator overnight. Heat through in a saucepan, stirring occasionally and adding a little broth if necessary.*

CURRY CHICKEN STEW

My Grandma Inky grew up in India and passed this recipe down to my mother, who then passed it down to me. I tweaked the ingredients a bit to fit my toddler's taste buds, but it's just as scrumptious as the original. This recipe brings back fond memories of my family gathered around the table.

—TERESA FLOWERS SACRAMENTO, CA

PREP: 15 MIN. • **COOK:** 4 HOURS • **MAKES:** 6 SERVINGS

- 2 **cans (14½ ounces each) chicken broth**
- 1 **can (10¾ ounces) condensed cream of chicken soup, undiluted**
- 1 **tub Knorr concentrated chicken stock**
- 4 **garlic cloves, minced**
- 1 **tablespoon curry powder**
- ¼ **teaspoon salt**
- ¼ **teaspoon cayenne pepper**
- ¼ **teaspoon pepper**
- 6 **boneless skinless chicken breasts (6 ounces each)**
- 1 **medium green pepper, cut into thin strips**
- 1 **medium onion, thinly sliced**
  Hot cooked rice
  Chopped fresh cilantro and chutney, optional

1. In a large bowl, combine the first eight ingredients. Place chicken, green pepper and onion in a 5- or 6-qt. slow cooker; pour the broth mixture over top. Cook, covered, on low for 4-5 hours or until the chicken and vegetables are tender.

2. Remove the chicken and cool slightly. Cut or shred meat into bite-size pieces and return to slow cooker; heat through. Serve with rice. If desired, top with cilantro and chutney.

HELPFUL HINT

Curry powder isn't a single spice; it's a blend that may have up to 20 ingredients depending on its place of origin. Curry powder is labeled mild or hot—your choice! You can add more curry to up the spice level; remember the flavor will intensify with cooking.

VEGETARIAN CHILI OLE!

I combine the ingredients for this chili the night before, start my trusty slow cooker in the morning and come home to a rich, spicy meal at night.

—MARJORIE AU HONOLULU, HI

PREP: 35 MIN. • **COOK:** 6 HOURS • **MAKES:** 7 SERVINGS

- 1 **can (16 ounces) kidney beans, rinsed and drained**
- 1 **can (15 ounces) black beans, rinsed and drained**
- 1 **can (14½ ounces) diced tomatoes, undrained**
- 1½ **cups frozen corn**
- 1 **large onion, chopped**
- 1 **medium zucchini, chopped**
- 1 **medium sweet red pepper, chopped**
- 1 **can (4 ounces) chopped green chilies**
- 1 **ounce Mexican chocolate, chopped**
- 1 **cup water**
- 1 **can (6 ounces) tomato paste**
- 1 **tablespoon cornmeal**
- 1 **tablespoon chili powder**
- ½ **teaspoon salt**
- ½ **teaspoon dried oregano**
- ½ **teaspoon ground cumin**
- ¼ **teaspoon hot pepper sauce, optional**
  Optional toppings: diced tomatoes, chopped green onions and crumbled queso fresco

1. In a 4-qt. slow cooker, combine the first nine ingredients. Combine water, tomato paste, cornmeal, chili powder, salt, oregano, cumin and pepper sauce if desired until smooth; stir into the slow cooker. Cover and cook on low for 6-8 hours or until the vegetables are tender.

2. Serve with toppings of your choice.

WEST AFRICAN CHICKEN STEW

I really love authentic African flavors, but they can be hard to come by in the U.S. This recipe features a delicious combination of readily available African ingredients like peanut butter, sweet potatoes and black-eyed peas.

—MICHAEL COHEN LOS ANGELES, CA

PREP: 20 MIN. • **COOK:** 30 MIN.
MAKES: 8 SERVINGS (2½ QUARTS)

- 1 **pound boneless skinless chicken breasts, cut into 1-inch cubes**
- ½ **teaspoon salt**
- ¼ **teaspoon pepper**
- 3 **teaspoons canola oil, divided**
- 1 **medium onion, thinly sliced**
- 6 **garlic cloves, minced**
- 2 **tablespoons minced fresh gingerroot**
- 2 **cans (15½ ounces each) black-eyed peas, rinsed and drained**
- 1 **can (28 ounces) crushed tomatoes**
- 1 **large sweet potato, peeled and cut into 1-inch cubes**
- 1 **cup reduced-sodium chicken broth**
- ¼ **cup creamy peanut butter**
- 1½ **teaspoons minced fresh thyme or ½ teaspoon dried thyme, divided**
- ¼ **teaspoon cayenne pepper**
  Hot cooked brown rice, optional

1. Sprinkle chicken with salt and pepper. In a Dutch oven, cook the chicken over medium heat in 2 teaspoons oil for 4-6 minutes or until no longer pink; remove and set aside.

2. In the same pot, saute onion in remaining oil until tender. Add garlic and ginger; cook 1 minute longer.

3. Stir in peas, tomatoes, sweet potato, broth, peanut butter, 1¼ teaspoons thyme and cayenne. Bring to a boil. Reduce heat; cover and simmer for 15-20 minutes or until the potato is tender. Add the chicken; heat through.

4. Serve with rice if desired. Sprinkle with the remaining thyme.

HELPFUL HINT

You can adjust your soup's thickness by how you treat your beans. Mash some of the beans, as in this recipe, or leave them whole for a clearer broth. For a thick texture, remove some beans from the cooked soup, puree them, and return them to the pot.

EASY WHITE CHICKEN CHILI

Eating plenty of chili is one of the best cold-weather strategies for staying warm. We use chicken and white beans for a twist on the regular bowl of red. It's soothing comfort food.

—**RACHEL LEWIS** DANVILLE, VA

START TO FINISH: 30 MIN. • **MAKES:** 6 SERVINGS

- 1 **pound lean ground chicken**
- 1 **medium onion, chopped**
- 2 **cans (15 ounces each) cannellini beans, rinsed and drained**
- 1 **can (4 ounces) chopped green chilies**
- 1 **teaspoon ground cumin**
- ½ **teaspoon dried oregano**
- ¼ **teaspoon pepper**
- 1 **can (14½ ounces) reduced-sodium chicken broth**
  Optional toppings: reduced-fat sour cream, shredded cheddar cheese and chopped fresh cilantro

1. In a large saucepan, cook chicken and onion over medium-high heat for 6-8 minutes or until the chicken is no longer pink, breaking up chicken into crumbles.

2. Place one can of beans in a small bowl; mash slightly. Stir the mashed beans, remaining can of beans, chilies, seasonings and broth into the chicken mixture; bring to a boil. Reduce heat; simmer, covered, for 12-15 minutes or until the flavors are blended. Serve with toppings as desired.

FREEZE OPTION *Freeze cooled chili in freezer containers. To use, partially thaw in refrigerator overnight. Heat through in a saucepan, stirring occasionally and adding a little broth if necessary.*

HEARTY PUMPKIN CHILI WITH POLENTA

Feel free to make this healthy chili a day ahead. It reheats nicely, and the polenta stays good for a few days in an airtight container in the fridge.

—WENDY RUSCH TREGO, WI

PREP: 30 MIN. • **COOK:** 45 MIN.
MAKES: 6 SERVINGS

- **1 pound ground beef**
- **2 celery ribs, finely chopped**
- **1 medium onion, finely chopped**
- **1 small sweet red pepper, finely chopped**
- **2 garlic cloves, minced**
- **1 can (29 ounces) tomato sauce**
- **1 can (15 ounces) crushed tomatoes**
- **1 can (15 ounces) solid-pack pumpkin**
- **1 tablespoon plus 2 teaspoons sugar, divided**
- **1 tablespoon chili powder**
- **1½ teaspoons pumpkin pie spice**
- **½ teaspoon plus ¾ teaspoon salt, divided**
- **½ teaspoon pepper**
- **1½ cups 2% milk**
- **½ cup heavy whipping cream**
- **¼ cup butter, cubed**
- **¾ cup yellow cornmeal**
- **1 can (15 ounces) black beans, rinsed and drained**

1. In a Dutch oven, cook the first five ingredients over medium heat for 8-10 minutes or until the beef is no longer pink and the vegetables are tender, breaking up beef into crumbles; drain.

2. Stir in tomato sauce, tomatoes, pumpkin, 1 tablespoon sugar, chili powder, pie spice, ½ teaspoon salt and pepper; bring to a boil. Reduce heat; simmer, uncovered, 45 minutes, stirring occasionally.

3. Meanwhile, in a large heavy saucepan, bring milk, cream, butter, and the remaining sugar and salt to a boil. Reduce heat to a gentle boil; slowly whisk in cornmeal. Cook and stir with a wooden spoon 2-3 minutes or until polenta is thickened and pulls away cleanly from sides of pan (mixture will be very thick).

4. Pour polenta mixture into a greased 9-in. square baking pan. Let stand until firm, about 30 minutes.

5. Stir beans into the chili; heat through. Cut the polenta into six pieces. Serve with the chili.

HARVEST BUTTERNUT & PORK STEW

Cure your craving for something different with a savory stew that's tasty with warm bread. Edamame adds an interesting protein-packed touch.

—ERIN CHILCOAT CENTRAL ISLIP, NY

PREP: 20 MIN. • **COOK:** 8 HOURS
MAKES: 6 SERVINGS (2 QUARTS)

- ⅓ cup plus 1 tablespoon all-purpose flour, divided
- 1 tablespoon paprika
- 1 teaspoon salt
- 1 teaspoon ground coriander
- 1½ pounds boneless pork shoulder butt roast, cut into 1-inch cubes
- 1 tablespoon canola oil
- 2¾ cups cubed peeled butternut squash
- 1 can (14½ ounces) diced tomatoes, undrained
- 1 cup frozen corn, thawed
- 1 medium onion, chopped
- 2 tablespoons cider vinegar
- 1 bay leaf
- 2½ cups reduced-sodium chicken broth
- 1⅔ cups frozen shelled edamame, thawed

1. In a large resealable plastic bag, combine ⅓ cup flour, paprika, salt and coriander. Add pork, a few pieces at a time, and shake to coat.

2. In a large skillet, brown the pork in oil in batches; drain. Transfer to a 5-qt. slow cooker. Add squash, tomatoes, corn, onion, vinegar and bay leaf. In a small bowl, combine broth and the remaining flour until smooth; stir into slow cooker.

3. Cover and cook on low for 8-10 hours or until the pork and vegetables are tender. Stir in edamame; cover and cook 30 minutes longer. Discard the bay leaf.

ITALIAN BEEF TORTELLINI STEW

This was the first recipe I created on my own—it turned out to be a keeper! You'll enjoy this rich stew full of veggies, tender beef and a splash of red wine.

—TAMMY MUNYON WICHITA, KS

PREP: 25 MIN. • **COOK:** 1¾ HOURS
MAKES: 6 SERVINGS (2¼ QUARTS)

- ⅓ **cup all-purpose flour**
- 1 **teaspoon pepper, divided**
- 1 **pound beef stew meat, cut into 1-inch cubes**
- 3 **tablespoons olive oil, divided**
- 2 **medium zucchini, cut into ½-inch pieces**
- 1 **large onion, chopped**
- 2 **celery ribs, sliced**
- 3 **small carrots, sliced**
- 3 **garlic cloves, minced**
- 1½ **teaspoons each dried oregano, basil and marjoram**
- ½ **cup dry red wine or reduced-sodium beef broth**
- 1 **can (28 ounces) crushed tomatoes**
- 3 **cups reduced-sodium beef broth**
- 1 **teaspoon sugar**
- 1 **package (9 ounces) refrigerated cheese tortellini**
- 1 **package (6 ounces) fresh baby spinach**

1. In a large resealable plastic bag, combine flour and ½ teaspoon pepper. Add beef, a few pieces at a time, and shake to coat.

2. In a Dutch oven, brown the beef in 2 tablespoons oil; drain. Remove and set aside. In the same pot, saute zucchini, onion, celery and carrots in the remaining oil until tender. Add garlic, oregano, basil and marjoram; cook 1 minute longer.

3. Add wine, stirring to loosen browned bits from pan. Return the beef to pan; add tomatoes, broth, sugar and remaining pepper. Bring to a boil. Reduce heat; cover and simmer for 1½ hours or until the beef is tender. Add tortellini and spinach. Return to a boil. Cook, uncovered, for 7-9 minutes or until the tortellini are tender.

PEPPERONI PIZZA CHILI

Pizza and chili together in one dish—what could be better?
Fill folks up at halftime when you dish up big bowlfuls of this chili.
—JENNIFER GELORMINO PITTSBURGH, PA

PREP: 20 MIN. • **COOK:** 30 MIN.
MAKES: 12 SERVINGS (3 QUARTS)

- 2 **pounds ground beef**
- 1 **pound bulk hot Italian sausage**
- 1 **large onion, chopped**
- 1 **large green pepper, chopped**
- 4 **garlic cloves, minced**
- 1 **jar (16 ounces) salsa**
- 1 **can (16 ounces) hot chili beans, undrained**
- 1 **can (16 ounces) kidney beans, rinsed and drained**
- 1 **can (12 ounces) pizza sauce**
- 1 **package (8 ounces) sliced pepperoni, halved**
- 1 **cup water**
- 2 **teaspoons chili powder**
- ½ **teaspoon salt**
- ½ **teaspoon pepper**
- 3 **cups shredded part-skim mozzarella cheese**

1. In a Dutch oven, cook beef, sausage, onion, green pepper and garlic over medium heat until the meat is no longer pink; drain.

2. Stir in salsa, beans, pizza sauce, pepperoni, water, chili powder, salt and pepper. Bring to a boil. Reduce heat; cover and simmer for 20 minutes or until heated through. Sprinkle individual servings with cheese.

FREEZE OPTION *Before adding cheese, cool chili. Freeze chili in freezer containers. To use, partially thaw in refrigerator overnight. Heat through in a saucepan, stirring occasionally and adding a little water if necessary. Sprinkle each serving with cheese.*

CHILLED
SOUPS

GOLDEN SUMMER PEACH GAZPACHO

Since peaches and tomatoes are in season together, I like to blend them into a cool, delicious soup. Leftovers keep well in the fridge—but this dish rarely lasts long enough to get there!
—**JULIE HESSION** LAS VEGAS, NV

PREP: 20 MIN. + CHILLING • **MAKES:** 8 SERVINGS

- 3 **cups sliced peeled fresh or frozen peaches, thawed**
- 3 **medium yellow tomatoes, chopped**
- 1 **medium sweet yellow pepper, chopped**
- 1 **medium cucumber, peeled and chopped**
- ½ **cup chopped sweet onion**
- 1 **garlic clove, minced**
- ⅓ **cup lime juice**
- 2 **tablespoons rice vinegar**
- 1 **tablespoon marinade for chicken**
- 1 **teaspoon salt**
- ¼ **teaspoon hot pepper sauce**
- 1 **to 3 teaspoons sugar, optional**
  Chopped peaches, cucumber and tomatoes

1. Place the first six ingredients in a food processor; process until blended. Add lime juice, vinegar, marinade for chicken, salt and pepper sauce; process until smooth. If desired, stir in sugar.

2. Refrigerate, covered, for at least 4 hours. Top servings with additional chopped peaches, cucumber and tomatoes.

NOTE *This recipe was tested with Lea & Perrins Marinade for Chicken.*

CHILLED RASPBERRY SOUP

PREP: 20 MIN. + CHILLING • **MAKES:** 12 SERVINGS

⅓ **cup cranberry juice**
⅓ **cup sugar**
5⅓ **cups plus 12 fresh raspberries, divided**
1⅓ **cups plus 2 tablespoons sour cream, divided**

1. In a blender, combine cranberry juice, sugar and
5⅓ cups raspberries; cover and process until blended.
Strain and discard seeds. Stir in 1⅓ cups sour cream.
Cover and refrigerate for at least 2 hours.
2. To serve, pour ¼ cup of soup into 12 cordial glasses.
Top each with a raspberry and ½ teaspoon sour cream.

Family and friends enjoy sipping this
lovely chilled soup. I often use a sugar
substitute and reduced-fat sour
cream to make it a little lighter.

—AMY WENGER SEVERANCE, CO

CHILLED CORN AND SHRIMP SOUP

Hot days call for cool foods, like this refreshing soup. Both filling and flavorful, it uses the best of summer's bounty. You can adjust the seasonings to suit your own tastes.

—MARY MARLOWE LEVERETTE COLUMBIA, SC

PREP: 30 MIN. + CHILLING • **MAKES:** 4 SERVINGS

- ½ cup chopped sweet onion
- 3 tablespoons olive oil
- 1½ pounds uncooked small shrimp, peeled and deveined
- 2 garlic cloves, minced
- 1 teaspoon curry powder
- 2 cups buttermilk
- 1 package (16 ounces) frozen shoe-peg corn, thawed, divided
- 1 cup (8 ounces) reduced-fat sour cream
- 1 teaspoon hot pepper sauce
- 1 teaspoon salt
- ½ teaspoon coarsely ground pepper
- 2 tablespoons minced chives

1. In a large skillet, saute onion in oil until tender. Add shrimp, garlic and curry; saute 4-6 minutes longer or until the shrimp turn pink. Remove from heat and set aside.

2. In a blender, combine buttermilk, 2 cups corn, sour cream, pepper sauce, salt and pepper. Cover and process until smooth; transfer to a large bowl. Add the remaining corn and shrimp mixture. Cover and refrigerate for at least 3 hours. Garnish individual servings with chives.

NOTES

CHILLED SUMMER BERRY BISQUE

PREP: 20 MIN. + CHILLING • **MAKES:** 8 SERVINGS

4½ cups fresh or frozen blueberries, thawed, divided
1 cup unsweetened apple juice
1 cup orange juice
¼ cup honey
2 teaspoons minced fresh gingerroot
1 teaspoon grated orange peel
¼ teaspoon ground cinnamon
⅛ teaspoon ground nutmeg
2 cups (16 ounces) plain yogurt
Fresh mint leaves

1. In a large saucepan, combine 4 cups blueberries, apple juice, orange juice, honey, ginger, orange peel, cinnamon and nutmeg. Bring to a boil, stirring occasionally. Cool slightly.

2. In a blender, process the blueberry mixture and yogurt in batches until smooth. Refrigerate until chilled. Just before serving, garnish with mint and remaining blueberries.

A blend of yogurt and spices thickens this cold blueberry soup and tempers the sweetness. It makes an attractive and healthy first course for a summer menu.

—ARLENE KNICK NEWPORT NEWS, VA

HELPFUL HINT

To store gingerroot, wrap it tightly in a paper towel, and place it in a plastic bag in the refrigerator or freezer. Fresh, unpeeled gingerroot can be stored in the refrigerator for up to 3 weeks and frozen for as long as 2 months.

COOL TOMATO SOUP

It's easy to crave soup—even on a hot day—when it's chilled and filled with the fresh flavors of summer. Serve a batch of this tomato soup as an appetizer or a side.
—WENDY NICKEL KIESTER, MN

PREP: 30 MIN. + CHILLING
MAKES: 9 SERVINGS

- 4 **cups tomato juice, divided**
- 5 **medium tomatoes, peeled, seeded and chopped**
- 2 **medium cucumbers, peeled, seeded and cut into chunks**
- 1 **medium green pepper, quartered**
- 1 **medium sweet red pepper, quartered**
- 1 **medium onion, peeled and quartered**
- 2 **garlic cloves, peeled**
- 1 **tablespoon minced fresh thyme**
- ¼ **cup white balsamic vinegar**
- 4 **cups cubed bread, crusts removed**
- 2 **tablespoons olive oil**
- ¼ **teaspoon pepper**
  Fat-free sour cream, fat-free croutons and parsley, optional

1. In a blender, cover and process 1 cup tomato juice and half of the tomatoes, cucumbers, peppers, onion, garlic and thyme until chopped. Transfer to a large bowl. Repeat.

2. Place vinegar and the remaining tomato juice in the blender. Add the bread; cover and process until smooth. Add to the vegetable mixture; stir in oil and pepper.

3. Cover and refrigerate for 1-2 hours before serving. Garnish with sour cream, croutons and parsley if desired.

ICY OLIVE SOUP

PREP: 15 MIN. + CHILLING
MAKES: 6 SERVINGS

- 2 **cups (16 ounces) plain yogurt**
- 2 **cans (10½ ounces each) condensed chicken broth, undiluted**
- 2 **cans (2¼ ounces each) sliced ripe olives, drained**
- 1 **cup coarsely chopped cucumber**
- ½ **cup chopped green onions**
- ½ **cup chopped green pepper**
- ½ **cup sliced pimiento-stuffed olives**
- ⅛ **teaspoon white pepper**
  Seasoned croutons, optional

In a large bowl, stir the yogurt until smooth. Whisk in the broth. Add the next six ingredients; mix well. Cover and chill for 4 hours. Stir before serving. Garnish with croutons if desired.

When summer turns up the heat, I reach for this cool, refreshing soup. The color of the olives contrasts nicely with the creamy yogurt base.

—**THERESA GOBLE** MUSCATINE, IA

SO EASY GAZPACHO

My daughter got this recipe from a friend a few years ago. Now I serve it often as an appetizer. It certainly is the talk of the party!
—LORNA SIRTOLI CORTLAND, NY

PREP: 10 MIN. + CHILLING • **MAKES:** 5 SERVINGS

- 2 **cups tomato juice**
- 4 **medium tomatoes, peeled and finely chopped**
- ½ **cup chopped seeded peeled cucumber**
- ⅓ **cup finely chopped onion**
- ¼ **cup olive oil**
- ¼ **cup cider vinegar**
- 1 **teaspoon sugar**
- 1 **garlic clove, minced**
- ¼ **teaspoon salt**
- ¼ **teaspoon pepper**

In a large bowl, combine all ingredients. Cover and refrigerate at least 4 hours or until chilled.

BLACK BEAN ZUCCHINI GAZPACHO *Substitute 2 large tomatoes for the four medium. Add 1 can (15 oz.) drained rinsed black beans, 2 chopped medium zucchini and ¼ teaspoon cayenne.*

REFRESHING GAZPACHO *Increase tomato juice to 4½ cups. Add 2 chopped celery ribs, 1 finely chopped red onion, 1 each chopped medium sweet red pepper and green pepper, ¼ cup minced fresh cilantro, 2 tablespoons lime juice, 2 teaspoons sugar and 1 teaspoon Worcestershire. Serve with cubed avocado if desired.*

SHRIMP BLITZ

PREP: 15 MIN. + CHILLING • **MAKES:** 8 SERVINGS (2 QUARTS)

- 1 **bottle (8 ounces) clam juice**
- 1 **package (8 ounces) cream cheese, softened**
- 1 **bottle (32 ounces) tomato juice**
- 1 **package (5 ounces) frozen cooked salad shrimp, thawed**
- 1 **medium ripe avocado, peeled and diced**
- ½ **cup chopped cucumber**
- ⅓ **cup chopped green onions**
- 2 **tablespoons red wine vinegar**
- 2 **teaspoons sugar**
- 1 **teaspoon dill weed**
- 1 **garlic clove, minced**
- ½ **teaspoon salt**
- ¼ **teaspoon hot pepper sauce**
- ⅛ **teaspoon pepper**

In a blender, combine clam juice and cream cheese; cover and process until smooth. Pour into a large serving bowl. Stir in the remaining ingredients. Cover and chill for at least 4 hours.

On a hot summer day, this refreshing soup really hits the spot. I've made it for special-occasion luncheons as well as for casual dinners with friends.

—JEANNETTE AIELLO PLACERVILLE, CA

CHILLED PEA SOUP SHOOTERS

Enjoy pea soup in a whole new way! The garnish is curried crab, which will catch everyone by surprise.

—*TASTE OF HOME* TEST KITCHEN

PREP: 20 MIN. + CHILLING • **MAKES:** 2 DOZEN

- 1 **package (16 ounces) frozen peas, thawed**
- 1 **cup chicken broth**
- ¼ **cup minced fresh mint**
- 1 **tablespoon lime juice**
- 1 **teaspoon ground cumin**
- ¼ **teaspoon salt**
- 1½ **cups plain yogurt**

CURRIED CRAB

- 2 **tablespoons minced fresh mint**
- 4 **teaspoons lime juice**
- 4 **teaspoons canola oil**
- 2 **teaspoons red curry paste**
- ⅛ **teaspoon salt**
- 1 **cup lump crabmeat, drained**

1. Place the peas, broth, mint, lime juice, cumin and salt in a blender. Cover and process until smooth. Add yogurt; process until blended. Refrigerate for at least 1 hour.

2. Meanwhile, in a small bowl, whisk mint, lime juice, oil, curry paste and salt. Add crabmeat; toss gently to coat. Chill until serving.

3. To serve, pour the soup into shot glasses; garnish with the crab mixture.

FROSTY MIXED BERRY SOUP

PREP: 45 MIN. + CHILLING • **MAKES:** 4 SERVINGS

- **1 cup sliced fresh strawberries**
- **½ cup fresh raspberries**
- **½ cup fresh blackberries**
- **1 cup unsweetened apple juice**
- **½ cup water**
- **¼ cup sugar**
- **2 tablespoons lemon juice**
- **Dash ground nutmeg**
- **1½ cups (12 ounces) raspberry yogurt**

1. In a heavy saucepan, combine berries, apple juice, water, sugar, lemon juice and nutmeg. Cook, uncovered, over low heat for 20 minutes or until the berries are softened. Strain, reserving juice. Press the berry mixture through a fine meshed sieve; discard seeds. Add the pulp to the reserved juice; cover and refrigerate until chilled.

2. Place the berry mixture in a food processor or blender; add yogurt. Cover and process until smooth. Pour into bowls.

As a lovely addition to a luncheon menu, our home economists recommend this cool, fruity soup featuring three kinds of berries.

—*TASTE OF HOME* TEST KITCHEN

HELPFUL HINT

If you don't have disposable gloves, an easy way to keep the oils from jalapenos off of your skin is to cut, core and seed the pepper under running water. If you like a spicier dish, keep some of the seeds and add them to the soup.

COOL WATERMELON SOUP

My refreshing gazpacho is a delightfully simple, elegant dish. Serve as a side or with pita and hummus for a meal.
—NICOLE DEELAH NASHVILLE, TN

START TO FINISH: 25 MIN. • **MAKES:** 4 SERVINGS

- 4 **cups cubed watermelon, seeded, divided**
- 2 **tablespoons lime juice**
- 1 **tablespoon grated lime peel**
- 1 **teaspoon minced fresh gingerroot**
- 1 **teaspoon salt**
- 1 **cup chopped tomato**
- ½ **cup chopped cucumber**
- ½ **cup chopped green pepper**
- ¼ **cup minced fresh cilantro**
- 2 **tablespoons chopped green onion**
- 1 **tablespoon finely chopped seeded jalapeno pepper**

1. Puree 3 cups watermelon in a blender. Cut the remaining watermelon into ½-inch pieces; set aside.

2. In a large bowl, combine the watermelon puree, lime juice, lime peel, ginger and salt. Stir in the tomato, cucumber, green pepper, cilantro, onion, jalapeno and cubed watermelon. Chill until serving.

NOTE *Wear disposable gloves when cutting hot peppers; the oils can burn skin. Avoid touching your face.*

SPRINGTIME STRAWBERRY SOUP

PREP: 15 MIN. + CHILLING
MAKES: 6 SERVINGS

- 2 **cups vanilla yogurt**
- ½ **cup orange juice**
- 2 **pounds fresh strawberries, halved (8 cups)**
- ½ **cup sugar**
  Additional vanilla yogurt and fresh mint leaves, optional

In a blender, combine yogurt, orange juice, strawberries and sugar in batches; cover and process until blended. Refrigerate for at least 2 hours. Garnish with additional yogurt and mint leaves if desired.

Laden with strawberries, this chilled soup is certain to become a new hot-weather favorite.

—**VERNA BOLLIN** POWELL, TN

CHILLED MELON SOUP

Looking for something to put pizzazz in a summer luncheon? Try this pretty, refreshing soup with a kick of cayenne pepper to get the conversation going.

—MARY LOU TIMPSON COLORADO CITY, AZ

PREP: 25 MIN. + CHILLING • **MAKES:** 6 SERVINGS

- ¾ **cup orange juice**
- 1 **cup (8 ounces) plain yogurt**
- 1 **medium cantaloupe, peeled, seeded and cubed**
- 1 **tablespoon honey**
- ¼ **teaspoon salt**
- ¼ **teaspoon ground nutmeg**
- ⅛ **teaspoon cayenne pepper**
- 6 **mint sprigs**

Place the orange juice, yogurt and cantaloupe in a blender; cover and process until pureed. Add the honey, salt, nutmeg and cayenne; cover and process until smooth. Refrigerate for at least 1 hour before serving. Garnish with mint sprigs.

NOTES

HEALTHY GAZPACHO FOR 2

Nutritious vegetables are the basis of this tasty chilled soup.
We recommend using spicy V8 juice for a zippier version.

—*TASTE OF HOME* TEST KITCHEN

PREP: 20 MIN. + CHILLING • **MAKES:** 2 SERVINGS

- **2 medium tomatoes, seeded and chopped**
- **½ small green pepper, chopped**
- **⅓ cup chopped peeled cucumber**
- **⅓ cup chopped red onion**
- **1⅓ cups reduced-sodium tomato juice**
- **¼ teaspoon dried oregano**
- **¼ teaspoon dried basil**
- **⅛ teaspoon salt**
- **1 small garlic clove, minced**
- **Dash pepper**
- **Dash hot pepper sauce**
- **1 tablespoon minced chives**
- **Chopped sweet yellow pepper, optional**

1. In a large bowl, combine tomatoes, green pepper, cucumber and onion. In another bowl, combine tomato juice, oregano, basil, salt, garlic, pepper and pepper sauce; pour the juice mixture over the vegetables.

2. Cover and refrigerate for at least 4 hours or overnight. Just before serving, sprinkle with chives and, if desired, yellow pepper.

SHRIMP SOUP

PREP: 15 MIN. + CHILLING
MAKES: 12 SERVINGS (ABOUT 3 QUARTS)

- 6 **cups (spicy hot) V8 juice**
- 2 **cups cold water**
- 1 **pound peeled and deveined cooked shrimp (31-40 per pound)**
- 2 **medium tomatoes, seeded and diced**
- 1 **medium cucumber, seeded and diced**
- 2 **medium ripe avocados, diced**
- ½ **cup lime juice**
- ½ **cup minced fresh cilantro**
- ½ **teaspoon salt**
- ¼ **to ½ teaspoon hot pepper sauce**

In a large bowl, combine all ingredients. Cover and refrigerate for 1 hour. Serve cold.
NOTE *This recipe is best served the same day it's made.*

Here's a refreshing take on the classic chilled tomato soup. Our twist features shrimp, lime and plenty of avocado.

—*TASTE OF HOME* TEST KITCHEN

CHILLED BLUEBERRY SOUP

With 100 blueberry bushes in my garden, I'm always looking for recipes calling for this sweet-tart fruit; I was so pleased when my granddaughter shared this one with me. It's a delightfully different soup.

—EDITH RICHARDSON JASPER, AL

PREP: 5 MIN. • **COOK:** 10 MIN. + CHILLING • **MAKES:** 4 SERVINGS

- ½ **cup sugar**
- 2 **tablespoons cornstarch**
- 2¾ **cups water**
- 2 **cups fresh or frozen blueberries**
- 1 **cinnamon stick (3 inches)**
- 1 **can (6 ounces) frozen orange juice concentrate**
  Sour cream, optional

1. In a large saucepan, combine sugar and cornstarch. Gradually stir in water until smooth. Bring to a boil over medium heat; cook and stir for 2 minutes or until thickened.

2. Add blueberries and cinnamon stick; return to a boil. Remove from the heat. Stir in orange juice concentrate until thawed. Cover and refrigerate for at least 1 hour. Discard the cinnamon stick. Garnish with sour cream if desired.

ALPHABETICAL INDEX